THE

Bernstein, Eleanor

THE   RENEWAL THAT
AWAITS US

THE Renewal THAT AWAITS US

EDITED BY ELEANOR BERNSTEIN, CSJ

AND MARTIN F. CONNELL

LTP

LITURGY
TRAINING
PUBLICATIONS

Acknowledgments

With the publication of this volume, the major addresses presented at the University of Notre Dame 1995 summer liturgical conference become available to a wider audience. The editors are grateful to the authors for their extra efforts in preparing these papers for publication. To staff members at the Center for Pastoral Liturgy, deep appreciation: Tim Fitzgerald, architect and chief engineer for the annual conference, and Nathan Mitchell, whose enriching conversation provides essential support for all educational programs.

This book was edited by Martin F. Connell, with assistance from Deborah Bogaert, the production editor. It was designed by Anna Manhart and typeset in Sabon and Gill Sans by the production artist, Karen Mitchell. Printed by Bawden Printing of Eldridge, Iowa.

Cover art: *Wedding Feast,* © 1996 by John August Swanson, serigraph, 17" × 25".

    Los Angeles artist John August Swanson is noted for his finely detailed, brilliantly colored biblical pieces. His works are found in the Smithsonian Institution's National Museum of American History, London's Tate Gallery, the Vatican Museum's collection of modern religious art, and the Biblioteque Nationale in Paris.

    Represented by the Bergsma Gallery, Grand Rapids, Michigan: 616-458-1776

    Full-color posters and cards of Mr. Swanson's work are available from the National Association for Hispanic Elderly. Benefits go to its programs for the employment of seniors, and to housing low-income seniors. For information, contact: National Association of Hispanic Elderly, 3325 Wilshire Blvd., Suite 800, Los Angeles CA 90010, (213) 487-1922.

Library of Congress catalog card number: 97-73207

ISBN 1-56854-087-6
NDNEW

To all those who dared to dream

    and to those who follow their lead,

    seeking and surrendering to the renewal that awaits us.

Contents

Eleanor Bernstein, CSJ

Introduction:

The Renewal That Awaits Us

In June 1995, at its annual national conference, the Notre Dame Center for Pastoral Liturgy launched a year of celebration marking the twenty-fifth anniversary of its founding. With the publication of this volume, the talks given at that conference have become available to a wider audience. We are grateful to the speakers who made those days lively and exhilarating. We hope that you will find their thoughts — now in print — provocative and challenging, and that they will spark good and fruitful conversation around critical issues in the renewal of liturgy and the renewal of the church.

Twenty-five years — roughly a generation. Where were you in 1970? Do you remember what Sunday celebrations were like in those days? Were you a student then, making you way through elementary or high school? kindergarten or college? Some among us were working for a coveted college degree; others were in the seminary or novitiate or graduate school. Many were beginning a family or a career or ministry in the church. No doubt many among us had already set about the radical work of changing familiar but outgrown habits.

Whatever the particulars, all of us were engaged — one way or another — in learning to live in a post–Vatican II church, where soon there would be more questions than answers, a great deal of hope and enthusiasm on the part of many, as well as skepticism and resistance in good measure. For all, without exception, it was a new time: There was a new church in the making, new work to be done and a new spirit moving the pilgrim people of God. We had begun a journey together! That was the context in which the Notre Dame Center for Pastoral Liturgy was called into being.

Now, more than a quarter-century later and a generation into the reform, even the most cockeyed optimists among us have left behind the exhilaration of those early Vatican II years. Sobered by the difficulty of trying to shape the dreams into reality, we have had to come to grips with the enormity of the task and the limits of our resources. Not unlike the disciples on the way to Emmaus, we too had high expectations. We had hoped that Vatican II would be the redemption of this new Israel: liturgy in the vernacular, the explosion of ministries, active participation, better preaching. . . . "We thought . . . we hoped . . . we expected." Still, we must remind ourselves that the road to resurrection always passes by way of Calvary: Ought not Christ to have suffered these things . . . ?

Nonetheless, we are sustained by an indomitable hope: The classic story ends with a promise to "make all things new." Disciples together, we journey into the future, to embrace the renewal that awaits us!

Anscar J. Chupungco, OSB

A Church Caught between Tradition and Progress

T he theme of this conference is a fitting tribute to the Notre Dame Center for Pastoral Liturgy as it celebrates its twenty-fifth anniversary: "See, I am making all things new" (Revelation 21:5). The renewal called forth by the Second Vatican Council led to the founding of the Center and has since guided it across the tension between progress and tradition, euphoria and wariness, and the uncertainties that mark these post-conciliar times. As we greet the Center *ad multos et proficuos annos!* we profess the conciliar faith that the Holy Spirit has not abandoned the eternal design to make all things new. The Center must live on to stand as a witness of the Spirit, who continues to infuse the church with renewed vigor.

"And the One who sat upon the throne said, 'See, I am making all things new.'" As I reflected upon these words, it dawned on me that they are emblematic of the things that accompany the process of renewal, namely: a prophetic vision, the tension that results from this and the summons to move forward. These are words that describe the vision of "a new heaven and a new earth," of a new city where God makes a home with people, of a new world that emerges in splendor as the old vanishes away. However, it seems to me that these words are also fraught with tension.

To make all things new, the former things must pass away, be put aside or perhaps even be destroyed. With awesome solemnity the visionary announces God's apocalyptic victory over evil: "And the sea was no more." Evil is symbolized by the sea where Leviathan dwelt, or by the sea that parted in two as the chosen people marched dry-shod in triumphal exodus. Finally, these words press us to move on in the assurance that God will fulfill the plan firmly and with determination. "Write this," said the One who sat upon the throne, "for these words are trustworthy and true." Indeed, as far as the Alpha and the Omega, the beginning and the end, is concerned, "It is done!"

Visions, tensions and challenges: These, it seems to me, are the three components of renewal that marked the Second Vatican Council and continue to diversely affect the postconciliar church.

Visions

In his address at the opening of the Second Vatican Council, Pope John XXIII reminded the assembly that it was not the principal task of the council to discuss church doctrines over again. "For such type of discussion alone," he said, "there was no need to convoke an ecumenical council." What needed to be done, he continued, was to translate the entire deposit of faith into words and actions that the people of today could understand and accept.[1] He repeated the impressive word *oportet* (it behooves) three times as he bound the church to a new mission in a world that had changed long ago.

We are familiar with the catchword by which he epitomized the Second Vatican Council, namely *aggiornamento,* or "updating." In every sector, the church needed *aggiornamento,* surely not by conforming to this passing age but, as our visionary explains, "by thrusting itself boldly and without fear in the work demanded by our time."[2] Thus on that auspicious morning of October 11, 1962,

Anscar J. Chupungco, OSB

Pope John XXIII shared with the world his fresh vision of a church in the modern world.

It was to be expected that *aggiornamento* would be the underlying motif of every conciliar document. We find this written on every page of the first document, the *Constitution on the Sacred Liturgy,* promulgated on December 4, 1963, under the papacy of another visionary, Paul VI. The document opens with the following prognostic words that, alas, are consigned to programmed oblivion by some sectors in our church:

> This Sacred Council has several aims in view: It desires to impart an ever increasing vigor to the Christian life of the faithful; to adapt more suitably to the needs of our own times those institutions that are subject to change; to foster whatever can promote union among all who believe in Christ; to strengthen whatever can help to call the whole of humankind into the household of the church.[3]

In its own way, a renewed liturgy can immensely contribute to the realization of this conciliar vision. That is why "the Council sees particularly cogent reasons for undertaking the reform and promotion of the liturgy."

The liturgy is not an empty ritual celebration; each liturgical rite, if it is adapted to the needs of the people of today, has a message to convey to the modern world. A renewed liturgy nourishes the spiritual life of the faithful, promotes Christian unity among the churches and contributes to the church's mission of evangelization. In short, the liturgy is a protagonist of the conciliar *aggiornamento*. Liturgical reform, ecumenical understanding and evangelization: These were the agenda of the liturgical movement; these were also the concrete reasons why Pope John XXIII convoked the council.

Although Pope Paul VI addressed the question of ecumenism and evangelization, he is best remembered for having courageously undertaken the arduous postconciliar reform of the liturgy. In his *motu proprio Sacram Liturgiam* of January 25, 1964, he writes that it has been "the concern of earlier popes, of ourself, and of the bishops of the church that the sacred liturgy be carefully safeguarded, developed and, where necessary, reformed."[4]

Time constraints and lack of expertise, with stress on the latter, do not permit me to dwell on all three: liturgical reform, ecumenical understanding and evangelization. Allow me then to consider only the first, with which I feel a shade less uncomfortable.

The *Constitution on the Sacred Liturgy,* coming as it did from this century's liturgical movement, has a monocular view of liturgical reform. We read in paragraph 14: "In the reform and promotion of the liturgy, full and active participation by all the people is the aim to be considered before all else. For it is the primary and indispensable source from which the faithful are to derive the true Christian spirit."

Participation is vital to the understanding of Vatican II's reform of the liturgy. It is the underlying reason why paragraph 21 of the *Constitution* desires that "both texts and rites should be so drawn up that they express more clearly the holy things they signify and that the Christian people, as far as possible, are able to understand them with ease and take part in the rites fully, actively, and as befits a community."[5] In the thinking of the council, active participation involves not only congregational acclamations, songs and gestures, but also, as paragraph 29 explains, those ministerial functions exercised by servers, readers, commentators and members of the choir.[6] The faithful take part in the celebration not only by being active members of the assembly, but also by ministering to its needs.

Participation persuaded the council fathers to finally approve the heatedly debated paragraph 36 of the Constitution, which still elicits either good cheer or annoyance, depending on who reads it: "Since the use of the mother tongue, whether in the Mass, the administration of the sacraments, or other parts of the liturgy, frequently may be of great advantage to the people, the limits of its use may be extended." Translation into the vernacular makes giant strides in articles 37–40, which outline the basic principles for inculturation.

In order to promote participation, texts need to be translated and their message communicated in the cultural setting of the audience. Thus translation entails inculturation. The postconciliar instruction *Comme le prévoit* goes so far as to assume that "texts translated from another language are clearly not sufficient for the celebration of a fully renewed liturgy. The creation of new texts will be necessary."[7] It would appear then that translation, inculturation and creativity are the three progressive movements toward the realization of the liturgical reform.

Devout and active participation, according to paragraph 50, is the primary end to be achieved in the revision of the sixteenth-century Tridentine Order of Mass. It is also the reason for which paragraph 62 boldly announced some long-needed changes in the liturgy of the sacraments and sacramentals. Finally in the chapters on the Liturgy of the Hours, the liturgical year, liturgical music, and liturgical art and furnishings, it stands out as the chief concern of the reform.

What, then, were the visions that urged the church, during and after the council, to work for the reform of the liturgy? It seems to me that when we speak here of visions, we are in reality dealing with the matrix within and from which the entire reform takes shape, namely full and active participation in the liturgy as source and expression of Christian spirituality. To promote it, the *Constitution on the Sacred Liturgy* envisaged the use of the vernacular, the revision and creation of liturgical rites, greater involvement in the liturgical ministries and inculturation.

Tensions

The visions I have pointed out were the ferment of change that stirred up the entire church a generation ago. Like many other changes of this magnitude, they drew forth contrasting reactions, and that caused division. For some, the liturgy must maintain its aura of timelessness in a world helplessly swept away by change. They regard any departure from the familiar way of doing things as a breach in the church's fidelity to its traditions.

We know that at the insistence, or perhaps under schismatic threats, of the Lefebvrian group, the Holy See, under the papacy of John Paul II, felt the need to issue the indult permitting the

Tridentine Mass, which in practice had been discarded by paragraph 50 of the *Constitution on the Sacred Liturgy.* Earlier, Pope Paul VI had reproved Archbishop Marcel Lefebvre for "the unlawful practice of celebrating the Mass of St. Pius V." In scorching words, he wrote to the archbishop:

> For you, the former rite of Mass is a sign of your false ecclesiology and a matter on which to assail the council and its work of reform. You take as pretext or as your alleged justification that only in the former rite are the authentic sacrifice of the Mass and the authentic ministerial priesthood preserved, their meaning unobscured. We reject out-of-hand this erroneous judgment and unjust accusation.[8]

Tension is fueled by liturgical romanticism in some sectors of the postconciliar church. As a lover of Latin and Gregorian chant, I consider it my privilege to repeatedly criticize their revival in the liturgy. To my mind, it indicates that there are people who have not followed the historical process. It is true that paragraphs 36 and 116 of the Constitution, given the peculiar circumstances prevailing in the council, claim them as distinctive elements of the Roman liturgy. It is true that the church of Rome has proverbially delayed the use of the vernacular, but it is part of its tradition to adopt the language people use in order to foster active participation.[9] To retrieve Latin as the language of the liturgy, regardless of whether or not the assembly can follow the readings and prayers, is to deny sound tradition and hinder what paragraph 23 calls "legitimate progress."

A subtle form of attack on progress is the kind cast by organized groups, like Credo, at the translations made by the International Commission on English in the Liturgy (ICEL). These groups take cover under the wing of "doctrinal concern," which smears the credibility of ICEL, of fidelity to original texts, which ignores the use of dynamic translation, and the inappropriateness of inclusive language.

The question of inclusive language in the liturgy is not an insignificant matter. It seems to me that the evolution of language is a cultural reality which the liturgy is obliged to accept; otherwise it will speak to people in a language that is far removed from their thought patterns. Thus, when we insist that God is a male person, we ignore the problem of biblical anthropomorphism. When we insist on calling women "men" or "brethren" and referring to our ancestors in faith as "fathers," we do not even pay lip service to the rightful place of women in salvation history and the life of the church.

However, there are two sides to a coin. While there are people who want the liturgy to be hermetically sealed off from the contemporary world, there are others who hold that the liturgy needs to be in constant dialogue with what goes on in the world and the church. They rightly claim that the liturgy, if it is to be an agent of renewal, should address today's cultural, religious, socio-economic and political issues.

One must admit, though, that exaggerations have marred the movement, compelling the Congregation for Divine Worship to issue on September 5, 1970, the Third Instruction *Liturgicae Instaurationes*.[10] The Instruction observed that there were people who, alleging pastoral needs,

> could not wait for the promulgation of the definitive reforms. In consequence, they have resorted to personal innovations, to hasty, often ill-advised measures, to new creations and additions or to the simplification of rites. All of this has frequently conflicted with the most basic liturgical norms and upset the consciences of the faithful. The innovators have thus obstructed the cause of genuine liturgical renewal or made it more difficult.

We of that generation need only recall the sudden apparition of newly composed eucharistic prayers, some of which can be censured for both content and literary form, the performance during Mass by jazz ensembles, the use of cookies and soft drinks for the eucharist, and so on. Wishing to curtail further abuses, the Congregation set down this rule whose tone is reactionary: "Any liturgical experimentation that may seem necessary or advantageous receives authorization from this Congregation alone, in writing, with norms clearly set out, and subject to the responsibility of the competent local authority."

In an effort to become relevant, some people entertain no scruples about allowing liturgical forms to be swayed by the modern way of life and values. The idea of "fast food eucharists" or 24-hour liturgies has become a subject of serious consideration; such notions are motivated by a desire to conform the liturgy to the situation of people on the move and to the declining value of family meals. What I see here is the failure to regard the liturgy as something countercultural, as a Christian critique of those modern values and institutions that weaken the human foundations of church and liturgy, such as community and family life, or that base themselves on the insidious premise that material and technological progress alone counts.

In the area of inculturation, some have integrated into the liturgy certain native rites of initiation, marriage and funerals that do not convey the Christian meaning of these rites, even if they do not contradict the church's doctrine. Often they are really nothing more than nice little tokens of cultural appreciation with no connection to the Christian liturgy.

In the process of liturgical renewal over the last 30 years, tensions have arisen regarding the proper implementation of the conciliar decrees. Even today there are people who receive changes grudgingly or, alas, simply resist them, and there are those who court the preconciliar liturgy with an attitude often deprived of historical and pastoral basis. These have time and again behaved like a terrier snapping at the heels of conciliar reform. The humility to accept an ecumenical council's decision is surely a more salutary attitude than a romantic adherence to the past, however glorious it might have been. However, I would not present an honest picture if I did not mention those who, driven by an unquenchable thirst for novelty, choose to ignore the right order of things. These are the recklessly euphoric who, unwittingly, give others reason to be wary of the conciliar reform.

Challenges

Visions generate tensions. Where do we go from there? In his address on October 29, 1964, to the members and *periti* of the

Consilium ad exsequendam, Pope Paul VI compared the liturgy to "a mighty tree, the continual renewal of whose leaves shows its beauty; the great age of whose trunk, with deep roots and firm in the earth, attests to the richness of its life. In matters of liturgy, therefore, no real conflict should arise between present and past."[11] In another address to the same body on October 13, 1966, he reminded them of the need to respect liturgical tradition. The criterion, he said, is what is best rather than what is new. "Nevertheless," he concludes, "the voice of the church today must not be so constricted that it could not sing a new song, should the inspiration of the Holy Spirit move it to do so."[12] In so many words, Pope Paul VI was challenging the *Consilium* to move ahead, to let the church sing a new song, yet not to forget, that the same church possesses "a priceless heritage worthy of veneration."

Much has been achieved since the promulgation of the *Constitution on the Sacred Liturgy.* But much remains to be done, even as the church, caught between tradition and progress, continues its pilgrimage amidst the changes and chances of this world. The following are a few points for reflection. I am sure that there are more and possibly more urgent ones.

1. *Conflicts among ethnic groups* resulting in genocide, armed strifes resulting in political tyranny, and socio-economic inequity resulting in poverty, murders and ecological destruction: This is the reality of the world in which the church moves, the reality with which the liturgy should dialogue if it is to be an agent of human renewal. But despair also casts its menacing shadow on the community of believers. There are Christians who fall away from the church or no longer talk to God because meaning and purpose in life have eluded them. There are Christians who commit suicide or euthanasia, because there is nothing more to look forward to in a life dominated by pain and suffering. This too is a reality with which the liturgy should dialogue if it is to be an agent of spiritual renewal. The question, then, is "Does the church have a liturgy that answers these human needs?"

2. Although much of its traditional components survive the test of time, *culture is in constant evolution* because new elements are

continually being introduced and integrated. Societies that have been traditionally agricultural are quickly shifting to industry. The *Fourth Instruction on the Liturgy*, issued by the Congregation for Divine Worship on January 25, 1994, is keenly aware of this. It calls for a balanced approach: "Liturgical inculturation should try to satisfy the needs of traditional culture and at the same time take account of the needs of those affected by an urban or industrial culture."[13] When we confine our attention to an agricultural liturgy, we exclude from our worship the concerns of a vast number of the faithful in urban communities. Unfortunately, our liturgy is still largely agricultural in its expressions. The question then is: Should we not perhaps consider a liturgy for people who live in an industrialized setting, where strikes, layoffs and the bargaining table play as important a role in the life of industrialized societies as the changes in the seasons of the year do for the agricultural world?

3. *The concern to gather the dispersed children of God* can be gleaned from both the conciliar and postconciliar decrees on Sunday assembly. Paragraph 106 of the *Constitution on the Sacred Liturgy* urges the faithful to gather together on Sunday so that through the word of God and the eucharist, "they may call to mind the passion, the resurrection and the glorification of the Lord Jesus."

The same Constitution exhorts that Sunday, which is the first among all the holy days, should "become in fact a day of joy and of freedom from work." We might note that in saying this, the council did not wish to make Sunday rest an absolute norm. From the conciliar discussions, we gather that Sunday rest was regarded as a matter of secondary importance compared to the Sunday celebration of the eucharist, which is what makes Sunday the Lord's day.

Today, in developed countries and among the middle class, Sunday has become part of the modern phenomenon called weekend. Weekend, which grew in some way from the observance of the Sunday rest, is characterized by tourism and recreation. This has caused the problem of absence on Sunday from one's parish and in many instances also of diminished participation in the Sunday eucharist.

But in situations of poverty, the observance of Sunday rest can become difficult. For the parish community, Sunday rest should not mean rest from works of love and social concern. The professional service of doctors, lawyers and teachers, offered freely to the poor of the community, should become a distinguishing mark of the parish Sunday observance. The Sunday assembly does not end in church but continues in parish clinics and classrooms. Lay leaders go about visiting the sick and the aged in order to bring to them eucharistic communion and the community's spiritual comfort. Once upon a time, the collection given at Mass in cash or in kind, as Saint Justin Martyr informs us, was set apart for the community's poor, widows and orphans.

What this is telling us is that the Sunday eucharist is incomplete unless it overflows into community service. Let us not forget that the promotion of social justice was one of the goals of the liturgical movement in the United States. According to paragraph 110 of the Constitution, social concern should be one component of our Lenten observance. The question then is, do we have a pastoral program that is able to translate into action the social thrust of the Lord's Day?

4. The reinstitution of the *permanent diaconate* and the *lay ministries* of lector and acolyte is a conciliar gift to the church. Even if, by some superior option, these ministries are reserved to male persons, they implement in a limited way the council's principle of full, active participation by God's people through active ministry.[14] I realize that I am treading on uneven ground. But we may wish to recall that our liturgical tradition, which does not know of women presbyters, knows of women deacons who received from the bishop the sacramental hand laying *orcheirotonia*. One prominent scholar denies rather easily that their ordination rite was not meant to be a sacrament. Other scholars, however, think otherwise.[15]

Documents as early as the third century speak of the ordination of women deacons. History attests to their ministry to the churches of Eastern and Western Syria, Chaldea and Persia, Egypt, Armenia, Constantinople, Gaul, Italy and even the city of Rome, at least by the end of the tenth century, despite the earlier prohibition by Pope Gelasius.

Around the year 1000, adult baptism gave way to infant baptism. This development caused the gradual disappearance of women deacons, whose principal role had been to anoint women catechumens during the baptismal rite. The question then is: Must the church consider the ordination of women to the diaconate a closed book?

The institution of women lectors and acolytes is, it seems to me, a slightly easier question. When Pope Paul VI issued *Ministeria quaedam* on August 15, 1972, he cited the "ancient tradition of the church" which reserved these instituted ministries to men. We know that because of their close connection to the liturgy, the ministries of lector and acolyte had been called minor orders. The clericalization of liturgical ministries, a movement that began with Pope Siricius in the late fourth century, resulted in their becoming a male reserve. Though *Ministeria quaedam* has extricated them from the clerical state, it continues to require them for the clerical *cursus*. This apparently is the reason for not instituting women to these ministries. Today women are allowed to be special readers, ministers of communion, and recently, altar servers, in keeping with their duty and right to share, where possible, in the ministry. The question then is: Given these progressive changes, would not Pope Paul VI smile complacently on the idea of instituting women as lectors and acolytes?

At the same time, I would like to direct attention to the post-conciliar gains the church has made in this area. Women are neither ordained deacons nor instituted as lectors or acolytes, but they may act as special ministers of communion, altar servers, readers and presiders at Sunday assemblies in the absence of a priest. In some local churches, bishops deputize women catechists to baptize solemnly. They also delegate women to assist as official witnesses at church weddings when no presbyter or deacon is present.[16] These then are some encouraging gains which we can regard as significant stirrings of progress in today's church. They tell us that progress in the liturgy can, indeed, be achieved without prejudice to our tradition.

5. *Inculturation,* formerly called adaptation, received a good deal of attention in the *Constitution on the Sacred Liturgy.* At a

time when some quarters in the church begin to be cynical about the present state of liturgical reform — think of the indult to celebrate the Tridentine Mass — the recent *Instruction on Inculturation* is a timely affirmation of the Holy See's continued adherence to conciliar decrees.

No doubt in some parts of the world, like the United States, inculturation will of necessity take on a multicultural dimension.

Imagine a Sunday assembly composed of people from various races, languages and socio-economic levels. A Hispanic sits next to an Asian. The underprivileged are mingled with the wealthy, the children with the adults, and no one feels like a stranger in one's home: They all belong; the *domus ecclesiae* is theirs. Different ethnic groups are allowed, even encouraged, to express the faith of the church in the language, rites and symbols of their traditional culture. Every member of the assembly is grateful for the experience of singing to the tune and rhythm of another's native music, is delighted to listen to the children's choir, is attentive to the announcement by an employee of a forthcoming strike. Yet, no ethnic group is hurt when told that a certain rite indigenous to one's country of origin, or a type of musical rhythm, is not appropriate to the liturgical celebration. Everyone accepts the fact that there are liturgical rules as well as cultural premises to be observed.

This is surely an idealized image of a liturgical assembly, but I think it aptly describes what inculturation means for a multicultural and multiethnic community.

The question then is: Are we ready for liturgical pluralism rooted in cultural or ethnic diversity? Will the pastor and community be comfortable with the Sunday Mass in which the different languages spoken in the parish are used? prayers in English, readings in Spanish, song lyrics in Filipino? Actually, the idea is not new. We know that until the seventh century, the liturgy of Rome was bilingual because of the migrants from Eastern Europe. Liturgy values hospitality. Greek *koine* and Latin were used for the readings on special occasions like Easter and Christmas, and for some rites of the adult catechumenate. Today, some of the solemn papal Masses, especially at the general intercessions, are carried out in a variety of tongues in consideration of the people who are present.

Another question is whether the pastor and community will allow the architecture and furnishings of the church to be influenced by native architectural and artistic designs. Viewed from one angle the *domus ecclesiae* will look African, from another Hispanic or European. It will not look like the traditional Gothic or Baroque church; it might not even pass for a postmodern building. What it will represent is not the fixed canon of church architecture but the image of a multicultural community gathered in worship, a sign of renewal in our divided world. The same observation will be made about the type of altar table, lectern, vessels and vestments. There is, of course, a principle involved here, namely the need to produce a sense of harmony among the different cultural symbols, a kind of unity among various elements, an eloquent symbol therefore of the multicultural and multiethnic community gathered together in common worship.

These considerations are another way of saying that in the sight of God and the church, all races and ethnic groups are equal. It means that all languages are suitable for the worship of God, that all musical forms, provided they enhance the liturgy, are welcome, and that all cultural rites and symbols, provided they harmonize with the true and authentic spirit of the liturgy, can be raised to the status of liturgical rites and symbols. To paraphrase a well-known line in George Orwell's *Animal Farm,* in the church, no culture should claim to be more equal than others.

Conclusion

"And the One who sat upon the throne said, 'See, I am making all things new.'" And the visionary of the Second Vatican Council said, "The church must thrust itself boldly and without fear into the work demanded by our time." And another visionary, who led the council to its conclusion, said, "The voice of the church today must not be so constricted that it could not sing a new song, should the inspiration of the Holy Spirit move it to do so."

Visions, tensions and challenges: These, to my mind, are the essential components of renewal. It is my hope that these reflections will, however modestly, assist us in assessing what has happened to the church and the liturgy for over a generation now, and in our planning on where to go from here.

1. *Acta Apostolicae Sedis* (AAS) L/V, 14 (November 26, 1962): 791 – 792. The following lines sum up this part of his discourse: *Oportet ut haec doctrina certa et immutabilis, cui fidele obsequium est praestandum, ea ratione pervestigetur et exponatur, quam tempora postulant nostra.*

2. Ibid.: *Sed alacres, sine timore, operi, quod nostra exigit aetas, nunc insistamus.*

3. *Constitution on the Sacred Liturgy* (SC), 1. In *Documents on the Liturgy 1963 – 1979* (DOL) (Collegeville, 1982): 4.

4. AAS, 56 (1964): 139; DOL: 84.

5. See also SC, 34, which embodies the classical ideals for active participation espoused by the liturgical movement: noble simplicity, brevity, clarity, comprensibility.

6. G. Shirilla, *The Principle of Active Participation of the Faithful in Sacrosanctum Concilium* (Rome, 1990).

7. *Notitiae* 5 (1969): 12; DOL: 291.

8. *Notitiae* 12 (1876): 417 – 427; DOL: 182 – 189.

9. See C. Vogel, *Medieval Liturgy: An Introduction to the Sources* (Washington, D.C., 1986): 293 – 297; Theodore Klauser, *A Short History of the Western Liturgy* (Oxford, 1979): 18 – 24.

10. *Notitiae* 7 (1971): 10 – 26; DOL: 159 – 167.

11. AAS 56 (1964): 993 – 996; DOL: 219 – 221.

12. AAS 58 (1966): 1145 – 1150; DOL: 223 – 226.

13. Congregation for Divine Worship, *The Roman Liturgy and Incultura-tion: Fourth Instruction for the Right Application of the Conciliar Constitution on the Liturgy* (Rome: Vatican Press, 1994): 30.

14. Paul VI, *Motu Proprio Ministeria quaedam*, AAS, 64 (1972): 529 – 534.

15. A.-G. Martimort, *Les diaconesses. Essai historique* (Rome, 1982); see, however, P. Sorci, "Diaconato ed altri ministeri liturgici della donna," *La donna nel pensiero cristiano antico* (Genua, 1992): 331 – 364.

16. The last two cases are covered by canons 861 and 1112 of the *Code of Canon Law.*

Nathan D. Mitchell

What Is the Renewal That Awaits Us?

Had I the heavens' embroidered cloths,
Enwrought with golden and silver light,
The blue and the dim and the dark cloths
Of night and light and the half light,
I would spread the cloths under your feet:
But I, being poor, have only my dreams;
I have spread my dreams under your feet;
Tread softly because you tread on my dreams.

— William Butler Yeats,
"He Wishes for the Cloths of Heaven"

I have only my dreams. I spread my dreams under your feet. Dreams are what I have to offer today. Dreams of where we've been (of the world that first dreamed *us!*), and dreams of where we might be going. "What is the (liturgical) renewal that awaits us?"

What is the Renewal that Awaits Us?

The question before us today is not *"Why did the renewal run out of fuel?"* but *"What is the renewal that awaits us?"* What we have been experiencing over the past thirty years was liturgical *reform;*

literally, *re-form*. For the past generation, we have been re-shaping texts and traditions (small "t"), music and movement, vesture and rubrics, seating and lighting, sanctuary arrangements, fonts and altars. We have been reacquainting ourselves with the basic requirements of ritual behavior — as fully conscious, active participants. *Reform* — that's what we've been about.

I suggest that we don't yet know what liturgical *renewal* will look or feel or sound like. *Renewal* is an event that awaits us — a becoming, an unfolding promise, a presence moving toward us that, when it arrives, will suffuse our hearts with wonder, shock and surprise. *Renewal* is that tempestuous, unpredictable experience the English poet George Herbert spoke of in his wonderful poem "Prayer":

> Engine against th' Almightie, sinners towre,
>   Reversed thunder, Christ-side-piercing spear,
>   The six-daies world transposing in an houre,
> A kind of tun, which all things heare and fear;
>
> The milkie way, the bird of Paradise,
>   Church-bels beyond the starres heard, the souls bloud,
>   The land of spices; something understood.

Reforms can be prophesied, predicted, planned and evaluated. *Renewals* cannot. Renewals can only be greeted, welcomed with humility and gratitude "in a lifetime's death in love" (T.S. Eliot). It is imperative that we not allow our arrogance — "we have all the answers" — to blind us to a future that may look, feel and sound very different from anything we can imagine today.

Recall the sage advice of Annie Dillard in her book *Holy the Firm:*

> The higher Christian churches — where, if anywhere, I belong — come at God with an unwarranted air of professionalism, with authority and pomp, as though they knew what they were doing, as though people in themselves were an appropriate set of creatures to have dealings with God. I often think of the set pieces of liturgy as certain words which people have successfully addressed to God without their getting killed. In the high churches they saunter through the liturgy

like Mohawks along a strand of scaffolding who have long since forgotten their danger. If God were to blast such a service to bits, the congregation would be, I believe, genuinely shocked. But in the low churches you expect it any minute. This is the beginning of wisdom.[1]

We must be on our guard against the danger of "creeping certitude." There are many among us today, in both church and culture, who are *very* sure about *very* many things. They are sure that God wants them to slay those "jackbooted government thugs" and to blow up federal buildings, day-care centers and all; they are sure God wants all good Americans to be armed to the teeth; they are sure that poor women on welfare should be scolded and punished; they are sure that poverty should be criminalized; they are sure that Rush Limbaugh is right; they are sure that Mother Angelica is right; they are sure that any film starring Arnold Schwarzenegger or Bruce Willis is virtuous and that any rap artist is drugged, violent and depraved; they are sure that health care doesn't need reform — and, besides that, only the shiftless, the lazy and the old get sick, and that's *their* problem; they are sure the Catholic Church would flourish again if only the Tridentine Latin Mass were restored, if only the laity wouldn't misbehave, if only nuns wore habits — if only, if only. . . .

The Embodiment of God's Grace in Jesus

You can reason your way into reform, but you can't reason your way into renewal. Reform is a rational achievement; *renewal requires an act of imagination.*

This suggests that ritual's role — liturgy's role — is not simply to remember but to re-educate. Ritual re-educates desire. Like music, painting, sculpture, poetry or the other human arts, ritual invites us to *dare* emotions — to *risk* feelings — we would otherwise never dare or risk. Ritual's role is to *awaken* us to new ways of knowing, naming and experiencing God. When those new ways begin to take possession of our hearts, renewal becomes a possibility.

We can't engineer or plan our way into the "renewal that awaits us"; we can only *dream* our way into it, *imagine* our way into it.

The question before us is not How can we reprogram the liturgical renewal, but How can we *de*program ourselves, open ourselves to experiences of faith and worship so new, so astonishing, so unexpected, that they can only be the result of God's Spirit, renewing the face of the earth. *Surrender* is key.

Remember that in the gospels, there is a story of how Jesus himself was shocked and jolted into a revolutionary new understanding of his mission and ministry. Jesus probably began his public life as a penitent, seeking purification and renewal as a disciple of John the Baptist. Together, they carried on *a reform movement within Palestinian Judaism,* calling people to repentance and to baptism as its sign. But somewhere along the line, something drastic happened to Jesus. He experienced a radical conversion that led him to break with John's reform program (to become an *apostate* from the Baptist's movement!) and, eventually, to reject the relevance of Israel's major religious and political institutions (temple, priesthood, monarchy). It wasn't that these institutions were irredeemably vile or wicked but simply that they had become (in Jesus' converted view) quite *irrelevant* to a person's relationship with God. Jesus stopped being a baptizer and became a healer, an "exorcizer" who liberated people from the physical, psychological and moral demons that possessed them.

> Why look . . . for someone to purify the repentant . . . when people already now know the restoring and compelling power of God's love? Why fast and pray when people are no longer anticipating a final purification but are already enjoying a gracious restoration of life? . . .
>
> Jesus does not any longer look for the kind of messianic figure, for God [is already, here and now] visiting and redeeming [the] people. . . . Jesus no longer seeks God in and through either performing religious ritual or calling upon the mighty to [repent and] perform deeds of justice, for he has found God and [God's] love in events in which the destitute, despised and despairing are restored to human society."[2]

One of the people who helped Jesus reach this conversion — according to a synoptic tradition recorded in Mark 7:24 – 29 and Matthew 15:21 – 28, its parallel — was a nameless Syrophoenician woman, a *Gentile,* whose child was in a desperate condition and needed healing. At first, Jesus rejects the woman's pleas with a sharp reply that appears to reject non-Jews from experiencing God's saving presence and power: "It isn't right to take the children's food and throw it to the dogs!" But the woman wittily persists: "Ah, yes! But even puppies under the table eat the children's crumbs!" The woman's retort repudiates the view that Jesus' power (as healer, as exorcist) is restricted to the people of Israel. Jesus himself seems stunned and moved by her wit, her insight and her persistence. The scene concludes with Jesus admiring this woman's *faith* (remember, she was not a Jew!) and with the child completely cured. (Note how Jesus' conversion comes from a completely unexpected source: a *woman!* an *"uppity" woman!* a *Gentile!* What a scandal! And what a clue for those of us who hope to make the move from reform to renewal!)

To sum it up, Jesus began as a reformer but became a healer, an exorcist, a *renew-er,* an embodied focus of God's forgiveness and grace.

An Excuse for Inaction

We need to stop invoking "reality" as an excuse for inaction. Reality is highly overrated. If Jesus had been a realist, he would never have made himself unclean by touching a leper; let his body be comforted by a sorrowing woman's gifts of kisses, tears and perfume; listened to the Syrophoenician woman; called the poor and the peacemakers "blessed"; or beckoned Lazarus from the grave. If Jesus had been a realist, he would have gotten an M.B.A. in Temple management and finance. If Jesus had been a realist, he would have spent that fateful Passover in Cancún. We have plenty of "realists" in the church — some of them even wear mitres and watered silk and carry big sticks. They are forever scolding us: "Be realistic! No singing! *'The People'* don't like to sing!" "Be realistic! Don't bother with the Easter Vigil—it's too long and cumbersome. *'The People'* won't stand for it."

I think the "realists" among us may need to listen to words that Jeff Behrens wrote in the *National Catholic Reporter* (May 12, 1995). Father Behrens was writing about the issue of "resources" in the church, especially the various campaigns to secure funding for projects like Christian education and vocations. He writes:

> The greatest resource that simply *is* the church is people. It is not what they have, or what they contribute, or even what they believe, that promotes the institution. I would prefer to bank on the treasure of human life and incarnate wisdom that is the average person. God speaks through people. The institution is given life, differentiation and tension through people . . .
>
> Millions have already been spent on vocation posters and campaigns aiming at an increase in ordained ministers. Meanwhile, from many corners there have emerged women, married and single people, who have expressed a desire to serve but have been alienated by the institutional stance on celibacy, power and women . . .
>
> I would suggest [that] our bishops take a year off. Take the millions that are raised, and take a long sabbatical. Go live anonymously among people. Live in apartments in cities, and keep your ears to the wall. *Live with families, and just feel, and listen, and suspend judgment. Feel in your guts how the very meaning of religion is being transformed, not by dictates but by the need of men and women to get along well rather than by platitudes or boring ritual.*
>
> The God the bishops speak so well of is in the street, in people, moving and breathing in all the richness of human life. It was this richness that so delighted Jesus, unless I have misread scripture. He found such great faith *in* people.
>
> Bishops: You will find, from people, that your world is far more confined than you think. You will discover that people do what they must as far as love, mercy and forgiveness are in human life. They are far more tolerant of you, bishops, than you of them, and perhaps a bit wiser. You may fear human weakness, including your own. They must come to terms with it every day. [Emphasis added]

The Holy in the Homely

The renewal that awaits us will unfold as we discover the Holy in the homely, the Divine in the daily, the light in the shadow, the sacred in the quotidian, the ordinary.

There is a passage in Nancy Mairs's wonderful book *Ordinary Time* that perfectly illustrates this point. Mairs argues that Christian ritual affirms a God with skin on, a God whose identity, whose reign or kingdom, can be known and named *only* as a leper's sores, *only* as a prostitute's costly perfume, *only* as a widow's hope for her dying child. Christian ritual celebrates the fact that the *holy* is known only in the *daily;* that the path to God is the path of *ordinary life.* It is the path of mewling children and pets that spit up on cashmere sweaters and neighbors with stereos from hell; it is the path of stained carpets and dying refrigerators; it is the path of sputtering marriages, adulterous affairs and failed resolutions; it is the path of AIDS and cancer and chemotherapy. That is why our rituals characteristically use the simple stuff of this world — light, oil, salt, water, bread and wine; hands folding in faithful promise; hands rising to bless; hands extending forgiveness; hands closing the eyes of death. *Ordinary life.* The holy in and as the daily. As Nancy Mairs puts it:

> Refrigerators and the wisdom or folly of their purchase do not belong in books about religious belief and religious practice, [so] convention tells me. Refrigerators are profane: [outside] the temple, not within its sacred precincts. God [is not concerned about] appliances.
>
> This kind of split makes me crazy, this territorializing of the holy. Here God may dwell. Here God may not dwell. It contradicts everything in my experience, which says: God dwells where I dwell. Period. I could give a clearer sense of this homeliness of the holy, I know, if I could make my mind up what I mean by "God." Instead, *I have to make God up, over and over again, adding fresh layers of comprehension, responding with new capacities for belief, in the protracted process I've come to know as conversion. . . .*
>
> God is *here.* And here, and here, and here. Not an immutable entity detached from time but a continual calling and coming

into being. Not transcendence, that orgy of self-alienation beloved of the fathers, but *immanence:* God working out God-self in every thing. *Process,* yes, that's what I want to explore and celebrate, *the holy as verb,* God*ing,* not Godness or Godhood. What she does. How she does it. . . . I'm certain that God slips and surprises more gloriously than Gerard Manley Hopkins's stippled trout.[3]

The homeliness of the holy: That is what Christian ritual recognizes and affirms. Liturgy invites us to *a new way of being human, together.* It's about joining the world — and loving it; it's about joining the human race — and loving it; it's about joining Jesus in the search for a new human community where rivalry, hatred and violence are overcome by partnership, love and life. Rituals are not perfect panaceas; they don't give us all the answers; they help us *learn to love the questions.* As the early Christian writer Tertullian once remarked, *Nihil humanum alienum a me puto:* "Nothing human is a stranger to me."

Liturgy calls us to embrace the full range of human experience — the warts and wrinkles, the vigils and dreams, the sound of water rippling over bone, the blood's breath, the light that shines from wheat and wood and honey, the sound of the words "night" and "goodbye." Ritual embraces even the heart of our lostness and despair, the harsh pain of consciousness, the tormenting truth of our loneliness and isolation — without rancor, resentment or bitterness. In the words of Etty Hillesum, a young woman who died at Auschwitz in 1943,

> How great are the needs of Your creatures on this earth, oh God. They sit there, talking quietly . . . and suddenly their need erupts in all its nakedness. Then, there they are, bundles of human misery, desperate and unable to face life. And that's when my task begins. It is not enough simply to proclaim You, God, to commend You to the hearts of others. One must also clear the path towards You in them . . .
>
> I have broken my body like bread and shared it out among [others]. And why not, they were hungry and had gone without for so long . . .

We should be willing to act as a balm for all wounds.[4] Clearing a path. Breaking the body's bread. Recognizing that the God *in* you desires God *for* you. Becoming human is an *art*. It's an art we *practice* by learning the ritual repertoire of the human community.

When we discover this truth, we'll be on our way to *renewal*.

The Next Generation

The first postconciliar generation was a generation of reformers — of librarians, text critics and translators, archivists and historians. The next generation must belong to the poets. (By this I don't mean the production of "self-consciously poetic texts.")

If we are to discover "the renewal that awaits us," we must rediscover the poetry of words and the poetry of motion. We need to rediscover a poetics of word and gesture, song and dance.

We need to learn (or relearn) that images arise before thoughts, that poems come before sermons, that the dance is older than the word. As the American painter Barnett Newman once put it:

> *The aesthetic act always precedes the social one.* The totemic act of wonder in front of the tiger-ancestor came before the act of murder. It is important to keep in mind that the necessity for dream is stronger than any utilitarian need. . . . [T]he necessity for understanding the unknowable comes before any desire to discover the unknown. [Humanity's] first expression, like [its] first dream, was an aesthetic one. Speech was a poetic outcry rather than a demand for communication. . . . [Our] first cry was a song. [Our] first address to a neighbor was a cry of power and solemn weakness, not a request for a drink of water. . . . The myth came before the hunt. . . . The God image, not pottery, was the first manual act.[5]

Poetic images thus have their own dynamic ontology, their own metaphysics — that is not based on cause and effect. Poetic images unfold not by means of causality (*this*, therefore *that*) but by what Gaston Bachelard called *"reverberation."* "In this reverberation," wrote Bachelard, "the poetic image will have a sonority

Nathan D. Mitchell

of being. The poet speaks on the threshold of being." In short, poems constitute "a metaphysics of the concrete." This metaphysics is based on the notion that "the essence of life is not 'a feeling of *being,* of *existence,*' but *a feeling of participation in a flowing onward, necessarily expressed in terms of time, and secondarily expressed in terms of space.*"[6] As Eugène Minkowski expressed it in his book *Towards a Cosmology,*

> It is as though a wellspring existed in a sealed vase and its waves, repeatedly echoing against the sides of this vase, filled it with their sonority. Or again, it is as though the sound of a hunting horn, reverberating everywhere through its echo, made the tiniest leaf, the tiniest wisp of moss shudder in a common movement and transformed the whole forest, filling it. . . .[7]

Poetic images can therefore create a *disequilibrium,* a thrilling sense of vertigo, a shuddering disturbance deep at the center of things that spreads outward to apprehend the whole range of reality and to alter our experience and perception of it.

Because of this, poems have a power to change us that sermons and theologies never have. In the deepest sense, then, a poem delivers "meaning" not by appealing to the intellect but by taking complete possession of the hearer's (or the reader's) being — and so demanding a complete change ("conversion") in life. Recall the concluding lines of Rilke's sonnet "Archaic Torso of Apollo":

> . . . here there is no place
> that does not see you. *You must change your life.*[8]

Or, as Gaston Bachelard expressed it:

> The image offered us by reading the poem . . . becomes really our own. It takes root in us. It has been given us by another, but we begin to have the impression that we could have created it, that we *should* have created it. It becomes a new being in our language, expressing us by making us what it expresses; in other words, it is at once a becoming of expression and a becoming of our being. *Here expression creates being* [rather than the reverse].[9]

Expression creates being. When we become discouraged that the reform "has not really taken hold," we have to remember that reforms *can't* "take hold" — not in the way images can and do. Only a poem can create "a new being in our language by *making* us what it expresses." That's why I've argued in this point that the "next" generation (the generation of *renewal*) must belong to the poets (and not, I might add, to the publishers of catechisms). For in poetic utterance, we discover that language is not simply an instrument, a tool for exploring reality and communicating the results of that exploration to others. Rather, language *is* reality, the point of emergence "in which life becomes manifest through its vivacity."[10]

Poetic images are thus not merely decorative flourishes; *they are mothers of invention.* Conceptual language requires centralization, the fixing of forms and meanings. But poetry "always has a movement, the image flows into the line of . . . verse, carrying the imagination along with it, as though the imagination [had] created a nerve fiber."[11] In a poem, we do not "grasp" an image; rather, we surrender to it. By abandoning ourselves to the image without reservation, we "enter into the poetic space of the image." Hence, a poem is not language as tool but language as *creator of reality.* We do not discover, control and define its images; rather, *we discover ourselves as formed, created, defined by them.*

> Otherwise
> the curved breast could not dazzle you so . . .
> Otherwise this stone would seem defaced . . .
> would not, from all the borders of itself,
> burst like a star: for here there is no place
> that does not see you. You must change your life.[12]

"A poem," as Andrée Chédid noted, "remains free. We shall never enclose its fate in our own."[13] The poet is thus one who *knows*, that is, one "who transcends and names what he [or she] knows. There is no poetry without absolute creation."[14]

The Future: A Global Church

In an address given to the meeting of Societas Liturgica in 1989, Aidan Kavanagh warned against the habit of identifying Christian community with the culture-bound, middle-class values of American "civil religion": Values such as "belonging," "participation in approved groups," "consumerism" and "comfort in affluence." When such values take over, Kavanagh warns, a "bourgeoisfying" of the church takes place. The middle-class is "ministerialized," community is reduced to a matter of "joining, meeting and speaking out," and the liturgical assembly moves away from the arts of ceremony and symbol "toward *verbalization* as the assembly's main medium of communication within itself." Under these conditions, Christian conversion, community and worship become "less an obedient standing in the alarming presence of the living God . . . than a verbose effort at raising the consciousness of middle-class groups concerning ideologically approved ends and means."

The church, of course, is not coterminous with contemporary white suburban middle-class American culture. It is a global church, a world church, a multicultural church, a communion of diverse communities where the vast majority of active members are the working poor. In 1900, 80% of all Christians were Caucasians who lived in the northern hemisphere. In another quarter-century, by the year 2020, this datum will have been reversed: 80% of Christians will be non-Caucasians living in the southern hemisphere. Already, the fastest growing Christian continent is Africa — and one of the fastest growing Christian countries is South Korea. [See Robert Schreiter, "What is Globalization?" Chicago: Catholic Theological Union, unpublished paper]. It doesn't take a rocket scientist to figure out that *globalization* is the church's future. This means, of course, that the church and its mission are in need of radical redefinition. For as pastoral theologian Don Browning notes, globalization is *not* about shoring up positions of power or about doctrinal defensiveness; it's about missions and evangelism. It's about ecumenical cooperation; it's about the dialogue between Christianity and other world religions; it's about the church learning from other cultures; it's about solidarity with the poor and oppressed; it's about the struggle for liberation, justice and peace.[15]

As Pope Paul VI insisted in *Evangelii Nuntiandi,* the church "exists in order to evangelize"; evangelization is "her deepest identity" (14). And what the church evangelizes is not simply "the world," but herself!

> The church is an evangelizer [Paul VI noted], but she begins by being evangelized herself . . . [S]he always needs to *listen* unceasingly to what she must believe . . . She is the People of God immersed in the world . . . often tempted by idols, and she always needs to hear the proclamation of the 'mighty works of God' which converted her to the Lord; she always needs to be called together afresh . . . and reunited. . . . [S]he has a constant need of being evangelized (15).

It is this larger vision of global church, of church as both evangelizer and evangelized, that should shape our efforts at helping catechumens understand their identity as Christians, their ministry as disciples and their destiny as citizens of the world.

Again, we'll know that *renewal* has begun when the church stops scolding everyone else and starts evangelizing itself!

1. Annie Dillard, *Holy the Firm* (New York: Bantam Books, 1977 [1979]): 60.

2. Paul Hollenbach, "The Conversion of Jesus: From Jesus the Baptizer to Jesus the Healer," *Aufstieg und Niedergang der römischen Welt* 25:1 (1982): 216–217; text slightly altered for inclusive language.

3. Nancy Mairs, *Ordinary Time: Cycles in Marriage, Faith and Renewal* (Boston: Beacon Press, 1992): 10–11; text altered, emphasis added.

4. Etty Hillesum, *An Interrupted Life* (New York: Washington Square Press, 1985): 173, 195–196; emphasis added.

5. John O'Neill, *Barnett Newman: Selected Writings and Interviews* (New York: Alfred A. Knopf, 1990): 158–159; emphasis added.

6. Gaston Bachelard, *The Poetics of Space* (Boston: Beacon, 1964): xii, editor's footnote; emphasis added.

7. Quoted in *The Poetics of Space;* pp. xii–xiii, editor's footnote.

8. *The Selected Poetry of Ranier Maria Rilke,* ed. and trans. Stephen Mitchell (New York: Random House, 1982): 61.

9. *The Poetics of Space,* p. xix.

10. *The Poetics of Space,* p. xxiii.

11. *The Poetics of Space,* p. xxiv.

12. Rilke, "Archaic Torso of Apollo," trans. Stephen Mitchell.

13. *The Poetics of Space,* p. xxvi, note 1.

14. *The Poetics of Space,* p. xxvii, quoting Pierre-Jean Jouvé.

15. See Don Browning, "Globalization and the Task of Theological Edcuation in America," *Theological Education* 23 (Autumn 1986): 23–59.

Mary Collins, OSB

Beginning Again

The name Michael Mathis ascribed to this award is witness to the fact that there have been many *new beginnings* in the work of liturgical revitalization. Mathis was part of the preconciliar liturgical movement that reaches back almost a century and a half and which had many new beginnings along the way. His vision of a renewed life of Catholic worship laid the foundations for the summer liturgy program and for the work of the Center for Pastoral Liturgy. European priest-scholars traveled to South Bend summer after summer in the 1940s and 1950s. They came to teach a few hundred eager American clergy and laity what they knew about the church's public prayer and what they hoped for. Here — though the students and faculty reflect the postconciliar phenomenon of an activated laity — that work continues.

In this new generation, you are *beginning again*. On this morning when I am receiving the Michael Mathis award — for "lifetime achievement," as I told my sports-minded brother when he asked "what for?" — I am going to presume to tell you what I think this new beginning might well be about and why I think it is necessary.

Mary Collins, osb

This year — or next — the revised English translation of the *Roman Missal* will go to Rome for *confirmatio*. Although there is more to be done by way of refinement, the project of producing liturgical books is coming to an end. The work of producing liturgies — Sunday eucharists week after week, season upon season; initiation liturgies; Christian funerals — this work has no ending. But it can be done more or less well, as we all know. And we may unwittingly be doing it less well despite our best intention to do better. A study done here at Notre Dame reports that on average, 28 percent of U.S. Catholics are attending Sunday eucharistic liturgy in the 1990s. The study does not ask why, but we ought to wonder, not as sociologists but as worshippers who are also liturgical leaders and liturgical experts. This is surely evidence that we need to make a new beginning; this is a new moment in the church's relationship to this culture.

This past year my own research has led me to look again at the nineteenth- and early-twentieth-century liturgical movements. I discovered something I had never reflected on directly, though the implications of what I discovered have been undertone or overtone to much of my writing. Let me set these remarks in a broader theoretical context. Without tending to details, let me note only that I accept the cogency of social systems theory. That is, I believe that unconscious social dynamics, precisely because they are unrecognized, shape the interactions of the social body from generation to generation. The liturgical movement and the liturgical reform have been driven by such an unexamined political dynamic.

My ecclesiologist colleague Joseph Komonchak has been studying the prehistory of the Second Vatican Council.[1] In the course of doing so, he has described the strategies adopted by the papacy to construct the distinctively nineteenth-century ecclesial phenomenon we know as "Roman Catholicism." Curious that Komonchak did not name liturgical practice among the anti-modern strategies, I began my own investigation. It became increasingly clear that Prosper Gueranger's particular interests in liturgical promotion were best understood as anti-modern and that he worked tirelessly, aggressively, to convince the papacy that liturgical practice had social and political significance in post-revolutionary France.[2] In a subsequent generation, the Belgian priest-monk Lambert Beauduin articulated a comparable vision on the social and political utility of the liturgy in the church's fight to retain the laity's allegiance in the culture of modernity.[3]

In the social alienation rising as the culture of Christendom gave way for modernity, both Gueranger and Beauduin acclaimed liturgical order precisely as hierarchical order. And both men saw the liturgy as a useful path toward the reconstruction of an ideal but disappearing social order. The familiar, well-ordered world of the Roman liturgy — spiritual power at the top and docility among the masses — was uncritically presumed to be "the sacrament of salvation." Textbooks on the sacraments made ordination, not Christian initiation, the foundation of ecclesial life and action. Consider the anti-modern ecclesiological dictum: The church is not a democracy.

The liturgical reform of Vatican II reasserted the primacy of Christian initiation and gave baptized laity new dignity as the worshiping assembly. But we have continued to struggle with issues of good order in the Western church, now contending over strategies that reinforce hierarchical order in the assembly or minimize it in favor of the primacy of the assembly. I cite one example among many. As the Roman liturgical books have created space for the laity to understand themselves as authentic subjects of the church's liturgical action, alternate ritual strategies have made the local pastor's chair or bench into his *cathedra*. Laity authorized to preside in the absence of a priest — whether on Sundays or weekdays — have been forbidden the use of what was once functional furniture. A second chair must be set in the sanctuary for the lay presider. The empty chair — redolent of the cup of Elijah at the Jewish Passover seder — takes on eschatological valence as a symbol of the community waiting for its priest, of the sacrament of hierarchical order, of the path to salvation.

This contestation over claiming the best places in the assembly is spiritually sterile, even if it is the present preoccupation of many of us religious professionals. So preoccupied, we are in good company, for Jesus' first disciples disagreed about whether they had "arrived" or were to set out "on the road to Galilee" even after the resurrection appearances. Most recently, preoccupation with "good order" has corrupted our efforts to find suitable words for our prayer. We must say in our English creed that Jesus became *man,* not that he became *human,* lest there be a linguistic opening for the "ascent" of women to ordination. Compared to the vision of the way of salvation set out in the New Testament, all this preoccupation with place is pretty banal stuff, yet our communal public worship is being trapped in the banality. Who among us — people who care deeply about the public worship of the Catholic community — has not wondered, "My God, what are we doing here!"

So we must begin again. Even while we recognize the relentless presence of the political in our liturgical acts, can we attend also to the power of the beautiful? Let me contextualize my comments.

Liturgical worship is covenant memorial in its intention. And the covenant we have been given is one that draws us as a church into communion with the mysterious divine communion Jesus disclosed to us. That communion we name "holy trinity" has reached out and gathered us in, so we believe; but it is also sending us out into the world as visible witnesses to divine love: some as martyrs, some as teachers or prophets or healers, some as scientists or social reformers. The rich tangle of relationships we call the mystery of salvation is what we mean to celebrate with our eucharistic memorial and with the initiation rites that lead to the autistic liturgy. The relationships are a tangle. They do not lend themselves to clear and precise verbal formulae or to simply binary ritual strategies. They need, to borrow an anthropologist's metaphor, "thick" symbolic forms. The Baroque liturgical forms eschewed at Vatican II had such density; so also do the Melkite forms many Roman Catholics are finding an attractive alternative to what they are experiencing as Roman liturgical banality and sterility.

Let's look at some recent history in order to locate ourselves, to understand the aesthetic deprivation of the present situation and the need to attend again to the beautiful. In the years before the Second Vatican Council, the liturgical movement in France was hand-in-glove with the secular avant-garde art movement; French Dominicans in Paris were the link between the movements.[4] The modern avant-garde art movement was quasi-iconoclastic in its interest in "pure form" and its rejection of the representational. This secular "cultural revolution" seemed to offer religious artists a theoretical basis for dealing with the decadence of much Baroque church art.

Liturgical historians could hear in avant-garde aesthetic theory echoes of Edmund Bishop's judgment that "[t]he native Roman rite is marked by simplicity, practicality, a great sobriety and self-control, gravity and dignity."[5] Perhaps these two ideal visions of the modern artist and the liturgical historian were never consciously set together in syllogistic terms. Yet we recognize them in the statement of a reform aesthetic in paragraph 34 of the *Constitution on the Sacred Liturgy*: "The rites should be distinguished by a noble simplicity; they should be short, clear and unencumbered by useless repetitions; they should be within the people's powers of comprehension and normally should not require much explanation."

But does this aesthetic of pure form work liturgically? I think the evidence is accumulating that it does not. Anecdotal and statistical evidence can be found in the steady erosion of liturgical engagement, even by those who want to be engaged. But the issues are complex; they are not simply a matter of taste. Victor Turner's theory on how symbolic forms work to engage people is supported by the theory of French psychoanalyst Julia Kristeva on the way the human-person-in-process negotiates the demands of the symbolic and semiotic orders. And these theories from the human sciences are complemented by the recent work of sacramental theologian Louis-Marie Chauvet on the effective symbol as one which invites "self-recognition." An aesthetic that embraces thick, ambiguous, multivalent sensuous forms seems to hold more promise for Catholic worship than a liturgical aesthetic of clarity and pure form.[6]

Yet, if return to a Baroque aesthetic and the embrace of the Melkite are equally inauthentic for American Catholics in the Roman communion on the threshold of the millennium, and if the modern aesthetic is impoverished, what shall this church do when we want to celebrate the cosmic relationships we call the covenant of salvation, a covenant which sends us with a mission into the twentieth century? Discursive, didactic liturgy engineered with a view to controlling intra-ecclesial agendas is like a bare scaffold; the church needs a mysterious holy place, more obscure and more brilliant than ordinary life, more filled with the spirit of Jesus, within which disciples can gather to be renewed in faith, hope and love.

How do we who are academic and pastoral liturgical experts and authorities help the Catholic people to find a way forward in the continuing renewal of the church's public prayer? Is there something informed leadership can contribute to the next moment in the liturgical movement? Is there a place for "experts" at this juncture, when we acknowledge again just how dangerous a thing a little learning can be?

Italian political theorist Antonio Gramsci wrote about the role of the "intellectual" in the social process. Perhaps, in an effort to locate ourselves, we can draw on an interesting distinction he makes between the "traditional intellectual" and the "organic intellectual." "Traditional intellectuals" represent historical continuity and the ties of the community to its past formations. "Organic intellectuals" are the thinking and organizing element of emerging groups in the body politic who are effective precisely because they are also conversant with the tradition. If you made the connection for yourselves, determining that you are to be cast in the role of "organic liturgical expert" in the next act of the liturgical movement, I want to step in as casting director and recast you — perhaps with few exceptions — with the "traditional liturgical experts."

Why can't you and I have the exciting new leading roles? If Gramsci's distinction is valid, those who are the emerging church — the church of the young, the church that does not have strong identification with European formations and with cultural elites but has many creative artists in its midst and many new concerns in its heart — will slowly shape the new liturgical aesthetic. We are the generation wandering the symbolic forty years in the desert. We are evangelists charged with handing on as best we can "the mystery of Christ" within which the whole world lies, so that the next generations can imagine it, recognize it at work in their lives, find it believable and celebrate it in spirit and in truth. Provided there are new generations of believers who can recognize the church's message of salvation as credible, as good news for a new moment in human history, new richness of symbolic imagination and aesthetic form will yet be the Spirit's gift to the churches.

Meanwhile, evangelical conviction must inspire our liturgical catecheses — and our lives. Our liturgical homilies must breathe the Holy Spirit at work in the church and in the world. Our weekly liturgical planning must draw on our own best creative gifts to invite this contentious generation to new life in Christ and renewed life with each other. I hope you are ready to begin again, handing on what you have received.

1. Joseph A. Komonchak, "Modernity and the Construction of Roman Catholicism," in *Modernism as a Social Construct,* ed. George Gilmore, Hans Romman and Gary Lease (Mobile, Alabama: Spring Hill College, 1991): 11–41.

2. Cuthbert Johnson, *Prosper Gueranger (1805 – 1875): A Liturgical Theologian* (Rome: Pontificio Ateneo S. Anselmo. Analecta Liturgica 9, 1984).

3. Lambert Beauduin, *Liturgy, the Life of the Church,* trans. Virgil Michel (Collegeville, MN: The Liturgical Press, 1926).

4. See Mark Wedig, "The Hermeneutics of Religious Visual Art in L'Art Sacre 1945–1954 in the Context of Aesthetic Modernity" (Ann Arbor: Dissertation Microfilm, 1995); JoAnna Weber, "The Sacred in Art: Introducing Father Marie-Alain Couturier's Aesthetic," *Worship* 69 (1995): 3.

5. Edmund Bishop, *Liturgica Historica* (Oxford: Clarendon Press, 1918): 12.

6. Mary Collins, "The Form of Liturgical Prayer: The Challenges of Embodiment, Aesthetics, Ambiguity," in *Teach Us to Pray,* ed. Francis Eigo (Proceedings of the 1995 Villanova Theology Institute. Publication pending. 1996).

Mark R. Francis, CSV

Multicultural Worship: Beyond Cultural Apartheid and Liturgical Esperanto

Them here are few words these days that strike more terror in a liturgical minister's heart than the words "multicultural worship." I do not believe that the usual source of this fear is a lack of good will. On the contrary, most of those working in multicultural settings continue in this ministry because they have experienced its particular grace — the surprising movements of God's spirit that can only be felt when one is forced to give up the illusion that one is *in control* (something that should be obvious in all ministry but is especially important when crossing cultural boundaries).

But multicultural liturgy as an experience of Christian worship where people of different cultures feel welcomed — and a real part of the assembly — presents a special challenge. It is a challenge that calls into question our very identity as Catholic followers of Christ. It often brings into relief our "dark side," the perennial human quest for dominance and control over people who are "other," which besets people of all cultural backgrounds. Nevertheless, I am convinced that liturgy in a multicultural setting can also be the occasion for experiencing the awesome and life-transforming revelation of our God in Jesus Christ. Our God is always revealed as greater, more generous, more inclusive than we who are limited by our narrow vision can imagine. However, for the liturgy in a multicultural parish to be truly itself — what its etymology suggests, "a work of the people" — we *all* must undergo a process of conversion. The demands of liturgical ministry in such a setting call us not only to change our attitude about liturgical forms but to reorient the very way the parish community lives and works. How does the community establish priorities, understand authority and develop a way of working and living together respectful of the different styles and approaches to parish life that are influenced by different cultural backgrounds? Rather than beginning with a critique of the "product" of our liturgical ministry — the celebrations themselves — it is imperative that the starting point for a multicultural approach to liturgy be found *before* we come together to worship. We need to be conscious of the presuppositions (and the prejudices) we hold when we are in the *process* of preparing multicultural worship events.

In order to describe in more detail what such a conversion entails, I will first identify two conflicting tendencies or strategies that affect how we as pastoral agents see the relationship between culture and liturgy. These tendencies often unconsciously shape and limit our efforts to be inclusive in a liturgical setting. I label these tendencies "cultural apartheid" and "liturgical Esperanto."[1]

Two Tendencies: Cultural Apartheid and Liturgical Esperanto

Most of us are familiar with "apartheid" as the term used in South Africa to name the racist policy of the separation of whites from blacks and from people of mixed racial background. In a certain sense, the policy of separation of cultures is sometimes (unconsciously) carried out in multicultural parishes by well-meaning pastoral ministers. Cultural apartheid is practiced when those on the pastoral team have what might be termed a romantic respect for the cultures represented in the parish. This exaggerated respect causes them to want to limit the contact of the dominant group

Mark R. Francis, csv

with the minority groups out of fear that they will forget their customs and language and lose their identity. The greatest pastoral danger, according to people who practice cultural apartheid, then, is that of assimilation. The various ethnic groups need to be kept separate and "protected" from the dominant culture in order to guarantee the preservation of their culture and their way of life.

In some ways, cultural apartheid is a very traditional solution to a multicultural situation. The national churches established by Roman Catholics and other churches in the nineteenth century were formed to preserve the cultural identities of the European immigrants to the United States. Although the Tridentine *Ordo Missae* was to be celebrated exactly the same way in all Catholic parishes, the language of the homily as well as the style of both worship and parish life differed markedly from one national parish to another.[2] Germans, Italians, Slovaks, French, Hungarians and other European immigrant groups long maintained their own parishes and parish schools to preserve their identity in an often hostile U.S. culture that was distrustful of both Catholics and foreigners.

Today, there are also voices that question what is termed the "multicultural ideology," that which forces cultural groups together willy-nilly and rides roughshod over their customs and sense of the sacred. Alan Figueroa Deck characterizes the effect of a multicultural approach to Hispanic ministry as "devastating."

> What it means is that, in practice, the Hispanic communities do not find secure, inviting places of worship, and ministers to go with them. In the name of the church's multicultural reality, a fundamental moment in outreach, one that takes time and tender, loving care, is short-circuited. People are sent to the large multicultural parish that has two tracks or more and in some rare cases is "integrated." The sociological truth that people unite from a position of strength is in practice being negated by the multicultural ideology.[3]

It would be a misrepresentation of Deck's article to accuse him of espousing "cultural apartheid" or a simple-minded return to a former solution, the national parishes. What he is warning against is an *ideological* application of multiculturalism that fails to take the specificity of Hispanic (or other non-mainstream U.S. cultures) religious values and liturgical customs seriously. But his call for a separation — as necessary as it sometimes is — comes perilously close to raising such a separation to an ultimate good in itself. It can be interpreted by some to suggest that those groups in society who cannot unite from "a position of strength" must always shun contact with the larger society out of fear of being co-opted or submerged in the mainstream culture. It may be that such a strategy of separation is the best solution for the moment in the life of a given cultural group's interaction with U.S. society. Ultimately, however, it is a solution that will never be permanently satisfactory for the simple reason that acculturation or "culture contact" will happen whether we desire it or not.

The effort of maintaining a parish and liturgical life sealed off from the larger society is simply an exercise in futility. The second and third generations of today's immigrants will be influenced by the surrounding culture, both civil and ecclesial. They will speak English and will be influenced by the values and way of life of their non-immigrant peers. That there will be contact and change is inevitable. What is not preordained is the way this contact and change will take place. For example, while it is inevitable that second- and third-generation Hispanics will speak English, it is not inevitable that they will abandon Spanish. The church, through the medium of the parish, can serve as an important resource for fostering this process of acculturation while preserving the fundamental human and Christian values expressed by the minority culture.

What does this mean in terms of liturgy? Clearly, an attempt to re-create exactly what is done in the "old country" is bound to be both inappropriate and less than compelling to all but the most culturally isolated. The reason for this is simply that the points of reference that connect the liturgy with the life of the people in the old country are different here in the United States. This is true even among those groups we tend to lump together inappropriately as all the same. For example, it is not possible to celebrate Our Lady of Guadalupe in a "mixed Hispanic/Latino community" composed of Mexicans, Puerto Ricans and South Americans in exactly the

Mark R. Francis, csv

same way this is done in Mexico, since Guadalupe has a particular social and political reference for Mexicans that she lacks for other groups. Those who choose the hymns for *Las Mañanitas* (the dawn serenade to the Virgin on December 12) should be conscious of the fact that the specific references to Mexican political/religious reality may well be inappropriate given the mixed nature of the assembly. More general songs and new compositions — some in English perhaps — need to be considered.

Cultural apartheid, then, will never be a satisfactory solution for the long term, simply because it does not reflect the life of the people gathered for worship. This approach is essentially unfaithful to the movement of the Spirit in the present lives of those who come together to celebrate Christ. These lives, for all but the most segregated or alienated, are characterized by a multicultural reality that needs to be reflected in the liturgy. For it is in lives lived in the present moment that the Spirit of God is moving. We do not celebrate the liturgy simply to recall a historic past, no matter how inspiring. We come together for worship, gathering in Christ's name in order to discern how God is present in the here and now, in the conditions of the life we are living. And in many of our parishes, a determining characteristic of this life is its multicultural character. Celebrations intent on simply evoking the past are really little more than pious and superficial exercises in nostalgia that ultimately fail to connect us to the God who is constantly recreating our lives and "making all things new."

Liturgical Esperanto

The opposite extreme to "cultural apartheid" is what could be termed "liturgical Esperanto." Most people are familiar with the artificial language called Esperanto developed during the last century by the Polish physician and philologist Ludwik Zemenhof. He hoped to create an international language that could easily be learned by people from many linguistic backgrounds and that was capable of providing a common platform for communication since its vocabulary was drawn from Latin, Greek, Romance and

Germanic language roots. Esperanto's structure, spelling and syntax were also made simple to help make it accessible to people from a wide range of linguistic backgrounds.

Esperanto enjoyed some initial success as a language capable of bridging the gulf among people during the height of the jingoistic European nationalism of the nineteenth century. However, most observers would question Zemenhof's claims as to his creation's real "universality." It is telling, for example, that only European languages were used to form its root vocabulary. Although it still has some following in Europe and North America, it is fair to say that as a *lingua franca* for the world, Esperanto was not an overwhelming success. One of the principal reasons for this lack of widespread acceptance is the fact that Esperanto — as opposed to Spanish, English, Mandarin or Urdu — is not a "living" language. No one learns Esperanto at their mother's knee. It is an artificial construct in which no one "lives" in the same way people think, dream and pray in living languages such as French, Hindi or Bantu.

Parishes with multicultural assemblies often attempt to create or re-create their worship in much the same way Zemenhof set out to create a language. With the best intentions in the world, they think that if elements reflective of the different cultural groups in the parish are included in the celebration, then all will feel included and an integral part of the assembly. But this often arbitrary parceling out of cultural elements among the various ethnic groups of the assembly usually has the opposite effect — that of alienation. An altar draped with a *serape,* a Vietnamese folk dance at the presentation of the gifts and a Polish hymn to Our Lady of Czestochowa after communion does not constitute "multicultural liturgy." There are several reasons for this, and they correspond to the reasons for the widespread lack of acceptance of Esperanto.

First, the way in which the decision is made to include or exclude cultural elements needs to be examined. Were the Mexicans asked about the *serape* on the altar, the Vietnamese about the dance or the Poles about the hymn? Are these liturgical elements expressive of the way they interact with people from other cultural backgrounds? Clearly, if a central planning committee composed of Euro-Americans simply looks about for cultural elements that appear to *them* as representative and places them in the framework of a liturgy that is essentially no different from the "mainstream" liturgies of the parish, the committee should be prepared to hear legitimate accusations of tokenism. Just as Zemenhof developed Esperanto from European language roots and claimed that he was constructing a universal language, so liturgy committees often cosmetically alter a few parts of what is basically a North American interpretation of the Roman Rite to give a nod to cultural diversity. The celebration, for all the juxtaposition of cultural elements, remains essentially a "mainstream" interpretation of what Euro-Americans imagine that multicultural liturgy should look like. It usually lacks profound cultural resonance of any of the groups present because they were never asked what this kind of liturgy would look like to them. Thus, the process by which decisions are made are as important as, or even more important than, the content of the decisions themselves.[4]

Second, as with Esperanto—an artificial language divorced from any real experience of life—so a multicultural liturgy prepared without asking contextual questions will always inspire at best tepid enthusiasm. What are the real concerns about faith and life that are shared across the spectrum of cultural groups in the parish? Liturgy is never an exercise in abstraction if it is truly understood as the work of the people. A *sine qua non* for multicultural liturgy preparation is inquiring about the material conditions of the people and the tensions and positive interactions that exist among groups in the parish. Liturgy prepared without a sense of where people are often becomes as artificial as Esperanto.

I would like to propose five considerations to help guide liturgical preparation in a multicultural parish. Avoiding the two extremes of "apartheid" and "Esperanto" is not easy, but if we are to realize the potential for multicultural liturgy that is truly transformative, we must be attentive to the different ways in which these two extreme approaches to the challenges of diverse assemblies affect the way in which we confront the ministry of liturgy preparation.

Consideration 1:
Beyond the "Getting a Piece of the Pie" Mentality

If one begins a liturgical planning process with the premise that the liturgy is something to be divided up like a pie, with the size of the pieces corresponding to the relative size of the cultural groups within the parish, liturgy will always seem to celebrate cultural diversity first and our shared experience of Christ and God's Spirit second. It is a question of priority and emphasis. I am not saying that we are to ignore the various groups that make up the assembly when we plan liturgy. We need to be sensitive to the presence of the cultural groups in the parish as well as to the presence of those who have often been traditionally voiceless or invisible in our celebrations: women, children, people with disabilities and those of different social and economic backgrounds. These persons need to be considered and represented in liturgical ministries such as those of the reader, acolyte and communion minister.

If we begin with the idea that parts of the liturgy can be easily parceled out among the various groups of the parish, we are looking at the liturgy as a series of discrete ritual acts rather than as an integral act of worship. It is more helpful to begin with this question: "Why have we come together at this place and time to celebrate this particular aspect of the movement of God's spirit in our lives?" That is, we need to start with what we share rather than with what separates us. The way in which we celebrate this movement of God's spirit in our lives and our worship flows from this principle, not from how we comprehensively represent all of the cultural differences of the parish. Our tradition also challenges us to be careful regarding how we approach the act of worship — whether it be monocultural or multicultural — for when we gather for worship, we celebrate and proclaim our very identity as God's people. Therefore, when we come together as church in the liturgy, it is important that we know that our faith tradition makes important claims on us.

The very nature of the church calls us to unity. As the first letter of Peter reminds us, "But you are a chosen race, a royal priesthood, a holy nation, God's own people, in order that you may proclaim the mighty acts of God who called you out of darkness into God's marvelous light. Once you were not a people, but now you are God's people" (1 Peter 2:10, 11). We need to take this seriously: *Once you were not a people, but now you are God's people.* Because of Jesus Christ, we have a new identity and relationship with God and with one another. We assemble together because we have been convoked by Christ—we have been "called together" (the origin of our word for church, *ek-klesia,* means to be convoked or called forth) regardless of nationality, language or economic background. We come together because we acknowledge that Christ's suffering, dying and rising is not just an event of remote history but one which changes our current perception of the world.

As Christians we participate in the paschal mystery and see in it the pattern for our own lives. For this reason, our oneness in Christ is not simply good managerial policy or "political correctness." Rather, it is a unity that comes from those who have had an experience of the Lord that transcends human differences and puts these differences into perspective, including those occasioned by culture. When we gather as a Christian community, we anticipate and witness to that moment when God in Christ will be all in all, when people of every nation and culture will sit down together at the same table of equality and love at the end of time. It is important, then, that all involved in multicultural ministry be clear that their primary ministry is to help a diverse community celebrate the paschal mystery of Christ experienced here and now in a multicultural setting, not to celebrate cultural diversity as the object of our worship.

Consideration 2:
Learning to Acknowledge Cultural Differences

Having said that cultural differences are relative, it is important, nevertheless, to learn to acknowledge these differences and at the same time to be aware of our own limited perspective. The fact is, after all, that we can only proclaim Christ to one another in culturally specific ways, in a specific language and with particular cultural references. Our faith is not disembodied but finds its origin in the incarnation of Jesus Christ in a particular place and time; our faith proclaims quite wonderfully and scandalously that God chose to be limited by human history in becoming a first-century Palestinian Jew. By becoming like us in all things but sin, God in Christ proclaimed the Good News in a way understandable to human beings, using the limitations of human language and symbols to communicate God's love. We are deluding ourselves if we think that we can proclaim the Good News any differently than Jesus Christ did or that the way we live and proclaim the gospel is somehow unaffected by our culture.

What does all of this mean on a practical level? It means that we must be aware in our liturgical planning and other ministerial activities that culture influences the way in which people communicate and understand their world and their relationships. An example: With respect to communication patterns, cultural anthropologists have distinguished between two kinds of cultures, "high context" and "low context."[5] High context cultures rely on the environment and relationships as well as non-spoken communication such as gestures, facial expression, even silences. The spoken word is not the common or even the preferred way of communicating. Life-long friends in practically all cultures, for example, can communicate a great deal of information with a glance. Parents from Asia and some parts of Latin America can communicate a range of meanings to their children in certain circumstances by just one look, one gesture — from "I really love you" to "You're in a lot of trouble now!" There is little need for words when one can communicate this effectively without them.

Different from these cultures are the North Atlantic cultures, which, due to various historic factors such as the Enlightenment, tend to use words as the principal, if not the only, usual or normative means of communication. We tend to distrust symbolic communication as ambiguous or unreliable and prefer the verbal, especially in dealing with public communication. For this reason, anthropologists describe our culture as "low context": We tend to communicate with words rather than with nonverbal symbols. This obviously makes a considerable difference in preparing a liturgy — especially if there are both high and low context groups in the assembly. One group will tend to be comfortable with fewer words, while the low-context group will tend to want a detailed explanation of everything. Needless to say, the culture that gave rise to our classic liturgical traditions was high context. The classic Easter Vigil, with its panoply of primordial sacramental signs and gestures — blessing the fire, the paschal candle, immersion of the candidates in the font, anointing, eating and drinking — depends largely on these nonverbal signs to communicate the faith of the church and to contextualize the biblical texts and the prayers proclaimed.

Noting the differences between these high and low context cultures does not solve the problem of liturgical planning for diverse assemblies, but its does help explain why one group does not need the constant verbal barrage that the other group expects.

Consideration 3: Acknowledging the Consequences of our Different Historic Experiences

What does it mean to acknowledge different histories? First, it means that we must avoid assuming that the history of every cultural group in this country is similar to that of our own. My mother's family, for example, is Hungarian. Though she was born in this country, the first language she spoke was Hungarian because that was the language of the home. She was raised during a period in U.S. history when "fitting in" with the mainstream was very important. It was the era of the melting pot. It was at Catholic grade school that she learned English and became "Americanized" in order to fit into U.S. society. Though it was painful, this process of Americanization was supported by her parents, who were reluctantly willing to forget about the old country and abandon many of their customs and values in exchange for their children's "success" in this new world. Learning English and adopting U.S. ways was the price my grandparents were willing to pay for acceptance and economic advancement in the new society. Other immigrants from Europe share this same basic pattern of entry into the greater society.

The same cannot be said, however, of non-European immigrants. While the melting pot myth held out a reasonable promise of advancement and economic reward for my European grandparents, this was not the case for others who came to these shores. The "American Dream" proved to be more of a nightmare for many who obviously did not "fit in." Hispanic Americans were discriminated against for generations as second-class citizens. In some areas of the nation that were wrested from Mexico, they were treated as foreigners in their own land. For centuries the church discouraged priestly vocations from those of mixed Indian-Spanish ancestry, which now helps explain why Hispanics coming to the United States did not come with their own clergy, as had the European American groups. "Let them learn English" became the refrain of much of the U.S. church to ministry with Hispanics until the 1950s and 1960s. African Americans, brought here forcibly against their will as slaves, were shamefully ignored during the last century by a Catholic church preoccupied with waves of European immigrants. Even within recent memory, African Americans were denied entrance to diocesan seminaries because of their race. These sad reminders of the historical record serve as background for understanding why some groups in U.S. society do not look upon the melting pot and the church in the same way that many of our European ancestors did. We also delude ourselves if we believe that racism is no longer a reality in the contemporary U.S. Catholic church.

There is, scholars point out, a four-stage cycle that many minority groups experience in relating to the wider U.S. culture.[6] Many begin by wanting, first, to *accommodate* themselves to the United States, by wholeheartedly and uncritically embracing everything about the new country, from representative government to fast food. After this, *disillusionment* sets in once certain persons in the group realize that they will never be regarded by many people in the United States as real "Americans." This second stage is characterized by a pulling back or a separation from "mainstream" U.S. culture to re-evaluate and to find understanding and support from people who speak their native language and who share their view of the world. The third stage is one of *dialogue* with the other cultures — adopting those aspects of U.S. culture deemed helpful and refusing to assimilate others that are seen as contrary to one's real identity. Finally, the cycle finishes with a fourth stage, the *establishment* of a fixed or almost institutionalized relationship with the larger society.

Knowledge of this cycle is helpful for pastoral ministers who must be aware that there are times when all of the efforts expended on trying to bring certain groups together will be a frustrating experience. Those groups in their "separation" stage are largely composed of individuals who are busy coming to grips with their new surroundings and are looking to others of their own culture for clues as to how to maintain a semblance of one's identity in a largely alien world. At the present time, this cycle is helpful in describing many of the Asian groups who have come to the United States over the past 20 years. They are still negotiating their relationship with the wider society. Comfort with intercultural association exists at different levels, depending on the length of time the group has been in the United States.

Consideration 4: Multicultural Liturgy
Is Impossible without Multicultural Relationships

Christian liturgy is the celebration of a common life of faith, not a substitute for it. As *Music in Catholic Worship* reminds us, when we gather for the liturgy, we do not come together as if God has been absent from the rest of our lives.[2] In fact, it is that presence of God's spirit moving among us, in our homes, with our families, in the workplace and in the joys and sorrows of life that grounds our celebration and helps make it authentic. This liturgical truism is also applicable to multicultural liturgy. Unless a parish is willing to strive toward communication and cooperation among its various cultural groups, attempts at multicultural worship will always be unsatisfying and frustrating because the celebration would be enacting a liturgical lie. If the only time different cultural groups come together is to prepare and celebrate a liturgy, then the parish is not really acting as one parish but as many parishes.

Consideration 5:
Popular Religion Can Help Contextualize the Liturgy

The Constitution on the Sacred Liturgy describes the liturgy as "the summit toward which the activity of the church is directed and at the same time the fount from which all the church's power flows" (10). In claiming the centrality of liturgy in the life of the church, liturgists and other ministers sometimes forget that the water from the fount or spring located at these upper elevations flows to lower levels of the mountain as well. This same section of the Constitution reminds us that the liturgy does not exhaust the entire activity of the church, nor by implication does it exhaust all of the possible communal forms of prayer. Over the course of the implementation of the liturgical reforms, in a well-meaning effort to focus our energies on the liturgy we unfortunately paid little attention to the extra-liturgical prayer of the people that had featured so prominently in their experience of public worship before the Second Vatican Council. We are only now appreciating that in many ways, the novenas, holy hours and other devotional aspects of pre–Vatican II Catholicism helped shore up or at least contextualize the liturgy in a faith that God was present in all aspects of life. The devotional side of Catholicism can again serve as a healthy support for the liturgical life of a parish, especially one that is multicultural.

While eschewing the overly sentimental and individualistic element of traditional Catholic devotionalism, a multicultural parish may find in practices of popular religion ways of bringing the parish together. As an example, let me propose a particular celebration of All Souls Day. It is common Catholic practice to invite all those from the parish whose loved ones were buried during the past year to a special Mass on November 2. Our Catholic tradition of celebrating and praying for our loved ones who have died in Christ is based on our conviction that because of Christ, death does not separate us; we are still one with those "who have gone before us marked with the sign of faith." This belief transcends cultural differences; it is at the heart of the paschal mystery. Given this excellent reason for a multicultural celebration, how could a diverse parish celebrate this important day in the liturgical and popular calendar? What process could be employed to avoid some of the perennial pitfalls of multicultural worship?

Reading God's word is always the appropriate place to start. If the liturgy planning committee is truly representative of the parish, the reflections on the readings will help shape the celebration. For example, one of the Old Testament readings proposed, that from Isaiah 25:6 – 9, with its vision of God's care for all humanity, is a particularly powerful text for a multicultural assembly.

Another crucial step in preparing liturgy in this context would be to ask questions. Rather than going immediately to the sacramentary, I have found it very helpful and extremely interesting to turn to those present and ask how a particular feast is celebrated in their country of origin. This kind of conversation will sometimes revolve around practices of "popular religion" — the people's Catholicism that cannot be found in ritual books but which constitutes an important part of the celebration for many, especially Latinos. Through this kind of sharing, one learns to understand what many people are expecting when they come to church on that day and why many who at one time attended have stopped coming back. They miss something that speaks to the heart of their religious imagination. There is no need to try to imitate what was done in the old country. Rather, the challenge is to offer an interpretation of the popular religious tradition that may also be able to bridge cultural differences in the official liturgy. The following will serve as a concrete example.

Several years ago, in a parish in Chicago with a mix of Anglo, Mexican and Korean members, the Mexicans petitioned the pastor for use of the church basement for a more *típico* celebration of the *Día de los Muertos*. As many know, it is customary in parts of Mexico (as well as other places in Latin America) to take food to the cemetery on November 1 or 2 for a kind of picnic or vigil, with the recitation of prayers and reminiscences at the graves of loved ones. To many Anglos, this appears rather disrespectful, but in the Hispanic view, this is a way to honor the dead. It shows that we still belong to one another and that even death cannot prevent us from having a meal together. The Hispanic group at the parish wanted to invite parishioners to set up *altarcitos* (little altars) around the walls of the gym, placing on these altars photos or other mementos of those relatives who had died, along with candles and flowers. At first the pastor, an Anglo, was opposed to this, because he felt that it seemed rather superstitious and almost pagan. After a few weeks of gentle persuasion he relented, and the first year, after the parish Mass of All Souls, the Hispanics went to the gym and the community shared a kind of potluck dinner in company with these *altarcitos* after members of the community offered a short prayer for the loved ones of parishioners who had died. For those who attended, the event was quite satisfying, especially those who were not able to travel back to Mexico or Central America for the funerals of relatives who had died. This ritual gave them a way to publicly grieve. It helped give expression and communal support to the loneliness and sadness that accompanies the death of a close relative or friend.

The following year, the Hispanics asked to do the same thing. But this time, the pastor was more enthusiastic. Several non-Hispanics, Koreans and Anglos had dropped into the celebration and asked if they, too, could participate in the *altarcito*/potluck celebration following the All Souls Mass. The response of the parish to this celebration has grown every year and has become more and more multicultural. Attendance at the Mass has also increased. Parishioners have told me that this is one of the most successful of their multicultural liturgies during the year, that both the liturgy committee and the parish look forward to this annual celebration.

This experience demonstrates the importance of promoting a dialogue between the official liturgy and the practices of the people. This does not mean that the goal is to reproduce exactly what is done in the old country; rather, the goal is to adapt popular religious customs to a new situation. Because "popular religion" touches issues of faith and life, these practices often offer an entrée for people of many cultures to express their faith. It gives important support to the official liturgical celebration and provides an opportunity for the parish to assemble socially yet in a religious context, for a common purpose.

Conclusion

The five considerations of this paper might seem obvious to some, yet they are not exhaustive of what can be said about multicultural liturgy and the challenge of a consciously multicultural liturgical life. However, this challenge has enabled us to see more clearly the relationship between our local Christian communities and the whole church. The American bishops expressed it well when they called on us to be aware of our missionary call, a call that is not one-sided but dialogical:

> Even as we go out to other nations to announce the good news, we must remain open to the voice of the gospel speaking to us in a myriad of cultural and social expressions. We must be willing to welcome new immigrants into our parishes, to respect the cultural treasures of these newcomers and allow ourselves to be enriched and strengthened by their witness to the faith. In this we come to see more clearly how the local church expresses the life of the universal church.[8]

And as the Roman Catholic Bishops of Galveston and Houston stated so well:

> We cannot be content with diverse cultures simply coexisting at a respectful distance. The catholicity of the church demands that these diverse cultures engage one another in conversation and extended social and liturgical interaction.[9]

Steering the midcourse between the extremes of cultural apartheid and liturgical Esperanto, we can chart a good course. The voyage is always easier, however, when we realize who is really directing our sails.

1. For a fuller development of these terms, see my "Multicultural Worship: Steering a Midcourse between Cultural Apartheid and Liturgical Esperanto," *GIA Quarterly* (Winter, 1993): 18ff.

2. On the contrast between Irish and German American Catholic parishes, see Jay P. Dolan, *The Immigrant Church: New York's Irish and German Catholics, 1815-1865* (Baltimore: John's Hopkins University Press, 1975): 79–80.

3. Allan Figueroa Deck, SJ, "The Crisis of Hispanic Ministry: Multiculturalism as Ideology," *America* 163:2 (July, 1990): 35.

4. In this regard, see Maria Elena Gonzalez, "Parish Restructuring in Multicultural Communities," *Origins* 24:46 (May 4, 1995): 781 ff.

5. E.T. Hall, "Cultural Models in Transcultural Communication," in *Nonverbal Behavior: Applications and Cultural Implications,* ed. A. Wolfgand (New York: Academic Books, 1979). See also M. Hecht, P. Anderson and Sidney Ribeau, "Cultural Dimensions of Nonverbal Communication," in *Handbook of International and Intercultural Communication,* ed. M. Asante and W. Gudykunst, (Newbury Park, CA: Sage Publishing, 1989).

6. James Bank, "Multicultural Education: Development, Paradigms, Goals," in *Multicultural Education in Western Societies,* ed. James Banks and James Lynch, (New York: Praeger, 1986): 2–28; see also Robert Schreiter's theological reflection on this cycle, "Multicultural Ministry: Theory, Practice, Theology," *New Theology Review* 5:3 (1993): 6–19.

7. *Music in Catholic Worship* (1972), in *The Liturgy Documents,* Third Edition, ed. E. Hoffman (Chicago: Liturgy Training Publications, 1991): 277.

8. National Council of Catholic Bishops, *To The Ends of the Earth: A Pastoral Statement on World Mission* (Washington DC: USCC, 1986): 36.

9. Bishop Joseph Fiorenza, Auxiliary Bishops Curtis Guillory and James Tomayo of the diocese of Galveston–Houston, "The Local Church's Cultural and Ethnic Diversity," *Origins* 24:5 (June 16, 1994): 65, 67–70.

Sylvia L. Sanchez

The Hispanic Presence:

A Challenge in Worship

T he National Survey on Hispanic Ministry, conducted in 1990 by the National Conference of Catholic Bishops/United States Catholic Conference Secretariat for Hispanic Affairs, revealed that:

> Fifteen percent of the dioceses in the United States are one-quarter Hispanic; in 7 percent of the dioceses in the United States, Hispanics are a majority; in dioceses with Hispanics, 75 percent of Hispanics are Catholic; 61 percent of non-Catholic groups (other denominations) have a plan of prose-lytism aimed directly at Hispanics.

The Hispanic influence is leading to new faces and new places in and for worship. What is the impact of Hispanics on the American church, now and into the new millennium?

We need to ask ourselves three questions about the situation:

1. How are we responding to this presence (not only the Hispanic presence in itself but the presence of two cultures together in a given place and time)?

2. Where is this co-presence leading us? Is it dividing us or helping us to confront new challenges? One thing is sure: This is not a static situation; it will develop one way or the other. The choice is ours.

3. What are the challenges for both the dominant culture and the minority? Do we recognize what those challenges are, and are we even interested in finding out what they are? Again, the choice is ours.

Mercy Sister Maria Elena Gonzalez, president of the Mexican American Cultural Center (MACC), puts it clearly: "We do not control who receives an invitation. We can only control our own choices: to sit at the table with all others or to skip the banquet."

Skip the banquet. It is that serious, and the seriousness of this choice is perceived with a sense of urgency by all of us, both those in the dominant culture and those in the minority.

I will emphasize the words "both" and "together" because we tend to lean too much to one side or the other in terms of what we can offer to each other or in an effort to "tolerate" each other. We often hear the exhortations: "Learn from Hispanics; they have a lot to show you," or "You must do things as we do them in America." Such statements can and have been used for two very different purposes: to try to bring both cultures together (inculturation/assimilation) or as an excuse to give up on each other.

The fact is that both statements bear some truth, but neither depicts an absolute reality. Not all that Hispanics bring, and not all that we do in America (even in the American church), is good. The U.S. Bishops wrote in their 1986 pastoral statement *To the Ends of the Earth* that "missionaries brought not only their strengths, but also some of their weaknesses." We need to admit, first to ourselves and then to each other, that we bring both our strengths and our weaknesses.

We need not negate our differences but rather should explore them together and see what beautiful things can come out of this adventure. And indeed, we must believe that something new and beautiful will emerge, because our belief is not unfounded; rather, it is founded on the assurance of the Spirit within us and on the surety that Christ gives new meaning to what we are and do, to what we discover together in the same Spirit that leads us and calls us to be one in Christ.

Again, from *To the Ends of the Earth:* "The church must feel at home in each culture." How do we, the church, accomplish this? How do we make each other feel at home? It is not just a matter of making each other comfortable — it is more serious and more urgent than that. It is about sharing the same mission and the same Lord. Again from the same bishops' statement: "Mission is characterized not by power and the need to dominate, but by a deep concern for the salvation of others and a proud respect for the ways they have already searched for and experienced God."

Our attempts to dominate the other become obstacles to our discovering the newness the Lord is making in the other. This inclination to dominate is present in both cultures, but because the power to dominate exists in the dominant culture, this is where "colonial attitudes," as the bishops name them, are more commonly found.

A colonizing attitude on the part of the dominant culture is a weakness to be admitted and avoided. Fear of rejection on the part of Hispanics is also a weakness to be overcome. Both weaknesses lead to a stagnant faith that puts a halt to the common mission that we have been called to: bringing forth the gifts of our differences.

Being aware of each other's differences is also a gift as long as those differences are celebrated rather than tolerated. We all have, of course, basic human needs that are common to all cultures; but in each culture we find specific gifts and needs. Being "at home" with each culture means, in practice, that we need not only become aware of those specific needs but also come to realize that the care we give in the form of service and ministry is going to be different; it cannot be uniform.

How do we overcome these attitudes that divide us? We need to begin by taking each other seriously. This means believing that we are not a curse to each other but a blessing; that we are called not to ignore each other's presence, not merely to tolerate each other but to come together to the banquet, to be together as a eucharistic people. When are we going to take hold of this challenge and believe that, in the words of Mother Teresa, "Together we can do something beautiful for God"? Our decision to respond is nothing less than redemption at work.

"Together" does not mean doing everything uniformly or imposing one's way on the other. Neither does it entail ministering or worshiping physically together all the time. "Together" doesn't even mean liking everything about the other. There are things Americans do not like about each other; the same thing is true among Hispanics. There are aspects of this culture that the other culture is not going to like. Not even wives and husbands like each other all the time! We need to be very candid, however, about our dislikes. Do our dislikes need to be changed or modified for the sake or our common mission? Is it that I do not like something because it challenges me to change, because it threatens the status quo, or even because, subtly, I know that what I am really doing is rejecting a person that is not like me or does not do things as I do? Underneath these attitudes there is often a subtle arrogance that blocks the continuing work of redemption. It is the arrogance which thinks that God speaks like me, looks like me, is of my political party, of my social status, of my race, of my culture. In the words of Voltaire, "God created man to His image and likeness, and man has never ceased to return the favor!"

"Together" means working through divergences and allowing differences to facilitate our travel toward the ultimate goal. It is having a proud respect for the ways other people in other cultures have already searched for and experienced God through their own traditions.

Sadly, we need to admit that this is not always the case in our dioceses and parishes. We often put people down and criticize their ways and their traditions; sometimes this is done openly, sometimes very subtly. We put down a culture or a tradition when those from the "other" culture are not given the opportunity to take part in the planning and decision-making of the parish/diocesan ministries. Not with words but with our actions we say that they have nothing to offer, and we have all that it takes. This attitude is not only arrogant and presumptuous, it is contrary to the message of the Good News.

Sylvia L. Sanchez

Sometimes we get tired and frustrated, and we change our attitude from one of imposition to one of relegation. But if imposing is dangerous and unfruitful, relegating people is equally detrimental. As long as "they" do not interfere with the "normal" ways of the parish, it is okay. Because something is "okay" or something is not evil, is it automatically a good thing? Cannot good things be nurtured so that they can get better? Exploring and nurturing each other's traditions is a process that requires patience, consistency and long-term determination. It is essential if we are to avoid prefabricated concepts of the other culture and if we are to stop automatically putting down traditions that we do not understand.

Hispanics hold many traditions that have been part of their culture and faith for generations. These traditions are part of what and who they are; but most of them are unfamiliar to the American church. Processions, for example, are very much a part of the Hispanic faith experience, but many times these have been criticized or not allowed because "we are not used to processions here." Only when we care enough to go to the roots of an external action or rite and find its meaning will we be able to first understand and then perhaps incorporate it into our celebrations, thereby enriching ourselves and the church. Processions may be meaningless if we don't capture the sense of pilgrimage, of being a pilgrim church, a people that is always on the move, a faith that is not stagnant. Processions are also a sign of "walking with you," a sense of *acompanamiento*. It is not only "being with you" but "walking with you." And since processions are always for a religious event, the meaning has even more depth: "I am walking with you; we are walking together on our way to the Father, to our final destination."

For Hispanics, processions express very vividly what they are experiencing in their lives, and isn't that what liturgy is all about? Celebrating our own life experiences, joys and sorrows, bringing them to the Lord in offering and praise and letting the celebration of those rites permeate our whole life: That is liturgy!

The feast of Corpus Christi is a major celebration in all Latin American countries and also in Spain. When Hispanics come to the United States and do not experience these celebrations, they experience a sense of emptiness because traditions that were very much a part of them are now gone.

Posadas (images of the pregnant Mary and husband Joseph seeking shelter) is another popular Hispanic devotion. Have we looked at the possibility of incorporating the *posadas* into the Christmas celebration in our parishes here in the United States? Certainly this is worth exploring. Far from being trivial, it reflects deep faith expressed in a very specific action or series of actions. That "we've never done it here before" is no reason to reject it.

The *Quinceañera,* or celebration of a young woman's fifteenth birthday, is an old Hispanic tradition, particularly for Mexicans. Now we are calling it *Quince Años* instead of *Quinceañera* because we are beginning to see some interest among young men to celebrate this rite of passage. Although it could be seen as a variation of the Sweet Sixteen celebration, the *Quinceañera* is not only celebrated with a debutante dance in society but is also celebrated with a eucharist. The young lady, previously presented in the church at her confirmation and first communion, is now presented as an adult. In some cases there are exaggerations, even extravagances, on the part of the family. Nevertheless, if given the proper pastoral and liturgical attention, this can be celebrated not only as a very important rite of passage from being a child to becoming a young lady with new privileges and responsibilities, but also as an opportunity to affirm and enhance the importance of being woman and what women contribute to family, church and society.

Both American and Hispanic women have much to contribute to family, society and church if we explore our gifts together. On the one hand, the American woman has struggled not only to find her place in society but to be acknowledged and respected. On the other hand, the Hispanic woman — in her own way and in spite of *machismo* — has enjoyed a prominent place, a very special place in her society precisely for being woman.

I am not implying that the Hispanic woman already enjoys what the American woman has been struggling to achieve. What I am saying is that American and Hispanic women have accomplished much in their individual cultures, and if their gifts and experiences are shared, they will be able to accomplish much more.

Sadly, more and more violence is being experienced in Hispanic families, and one factor must be that the woman is losing her special place or that she is no longer accepting it. Here is a very clear example of the need we have to help and support each other to preserve, maintain and nurture the values of each other's culture.

I recently attended the ordination of a friend in El Paso, Texas, where Hispanic traditions were allowed and celebrated. Several things during the liturgy pleasantly caught my attention: The Mariachi choir in their traditional costumes, the very beautiful dance that inspired and invited us to deeper prayer during the *Gloria* and the psalm, and the fact that the parents of my friend had a prominent part in the liturgy, coming into the church hand in hand with their son and blessing him before they themselves received a blessing from him. All of this enriched and invigorated the church.

I am not advocating that all ordinations be celebrated exactly like this one. This liturgy was situated in the life experience of this particular family, its community and its cultural background. And not only was the family allowed to bring its traditions and diversities to the celebration, but those traditions and those diversities were welcomed and shared by others of different traditions. As a result, the church is now richer, as is each one of us who participated.

I feel privileged to work in the English and Hispanic communities simultaneously. One of the reasons I feel privileged and regard this as a gift is that I am able to see the richness in and the faith experience of both. I belong to a parish where liturgy is very much alive and liturgical celebrations are very well prepared, and the results are rich indeed. Liturgy, which embraces all of parish life, is where one can best appreciate and measure the vitality of the life of the parish community. I regard liturgy as a thermometer; it tells the temperature of the "body." Therefore, when I refer to liturgy, I am not only talking about the "making" of liturgy but also about the whole parish life reflected in the rites.

To illustrate some of these "principles" concerned with acknowledging and blessing the presence of diverse cultures, consider the following practices, which are used in my own parish.

1. The Day of Reflection in the RCIA was planned jointly and without fear of those from another culture. The two traditions accepted the challenge, and the result was a mutual blessing. We had decided that after a slide presentation, all would be asked to mention a phrase or word from scripture. Hispanics would respond in Spanish without translation. There was a great sense of freedom. And this is very important to accomplish, for freedom is also what liturgy is all about: The freedom to be who you are and worship your Lord as you are.

At the end of that day we knew, because we experienced it in the words and attitudes of those present, not only that this had been "okay," but that something special had happened. Christ had been in our midst. Christ the American and Christ the Hispanic, Christ speaking in Spanish and also in English, Christ pale and Christ dark: the Christ of many different traditions, yet one and the same. Because of that, we were all made new and renewed, both individually and collectively. In a very specific time and place we had contributed to a more holistic parish community, to a more holistic church.

When we plan together, we create a common vision with the added advantage of varied perspectives. What has been good for the Hispanic faith experience may be equally good for the American faith expression, and vice versa. Americans and Hispanics both can learn from each other and be enriched by each other.

Thus, what I am saying is that we need to overcome the fallacies that we have nothing worth offering or that we know it all and need nothing or no one else's presence to make us whole. Both extremes are demeaning for us personally and for the church community. Both attitudes are a block in our faith journey.

In addition, we must guard against the other extreme, which makes us feel guilty because we think that what we are doing in our own group is bad. This is not necessarily so. As a matter of fact, more than likely, it is "good." Nonetheless, if it is not inclusive of everyone, it is not complete, it is not whole, and consequently it is not the church. It is essential for us, the church, to think beyond our limits, to transcend the comfortable but crippling notion that just because we are doing good deeds we are already realizing our mission as church. We may be doing good deeds, but we have failed to bring all gifts to the altar! We have mutilated the body because if only some members belong, then it is not the whole body.

These fallacies, these attitudes, are not present in one culture more than in the other. As I said once before, it is more obvious and more common in the dominant culture because the power and the resources are greater there than in the minority. But this can be present in both.

2. Another example concerns the Easter Vigil, which has been restored in many parishes. However, Hispanics in general are not very familiar with this important rite of the church year. I am deeply joyful to see how Hispanics in my parish, as a result of very specific actions on the part of the liturgy commission of the parish, are being drawn to appreciate this central celebration of the liturgical year. Small steps can have far-reaching results when they are taken with a sincere, enthusiastic and wholehearted attitude to celebrate the oneness of the Body of Christ.

The Easter celebration in my parish was a bilingual liturgy, with both choirs singing English and Spanish songs together. The Hispanic priest prayed the eucharistic prayer in English, and the English-speaking pastor prayed his part in Spanish. Thus did the community acknowlege, proclaim and celebrate their oneness in the Lord.

There is yet much more to do in this positive direction. For example, I often wonder why there are only Hispanics at the celebrations of the feasts of Hispanic patrons or patronesses — feasts like Our Lady of Guadalupe, Our Lady of the Rosary of Chiquinquira, Our Lady of Charity. The English community is invited sometimes, but they are not really encouraged to participate. Hispanics usually want to plan the celebration, seeing it as "their thing," but in doing so they deprive the American church of their gifts. Americans are not naturally drawn to these liturgies because such celebrations have not been part of their upbringing and faith journey. Why don't Hispanics invite their American sisters and brothers to participate even in the planning of these liturgies? We all know that when we are involved in planning something, we learn a great deal about whatever that project might be. We've all heard that if you really want to learn something, teach it. How else are we going to learn from each other? There is only so much we can learn from a workshop, a video or any other tool of communication. (These are certainly good; they invite us and can certainly help in renewing our perspectives, concepts and attitudes, but we need to collaborate and plan together if we are truly to share and offer our gifts for the good of the whole.)

Challenges Ahead as We Move to the New Millennium

All of us have heard about plans, projections and goals for the third millennium: seminars such as "Recruiting Techniques of the 21st Century," "The Marketplace of the New Millennium," "The Impact of Ergonomics in the Third Millennium" and "The Environment at the Turn of the Century." There is even a car named after it!

How are we Christians going to celebrate what the pope has called "The Great Jubilee"? How are we preparing, particularly in Catholic churches? For us Christians, the celebration of this event has a deeper meaning because what we are celebrating is an anniversary of the coming of God into our midst in the person of Jesus Christ. Our celebration is rooted in the presence of God incarnate.

In his apostolic letter "As the Third Millennium Draws Near," John Paul II writes: "We need to approach this celebration with a sense of gratitude and yet with a sense of responsibility." Inasmuch as everything remains conceptual until it is applied, we need to consider our own reality, the reality of the American church, the reality of our dioceses, and even more concretely, the reality of our parishes in order for gratitude and responsibility to move from concept to application at a personal level and at a communal level.

One constant in the American church is the Hispanic presence, although that presence is different in each of our dioceses and parishes. It will be our responsibility to determine how we can respect, integrate and celebrate the diversity of gifts in this presence. As the American church moves toward the third millennium, we must press forward to discover the gifts of all those whom the

Lord has invited to the banquet. May we not skip the banquet on account of our differences, but rather make the decision to celebrate those differences.

John Paul II, in his apostolic letter on the "Great Jubilee," states that "during the Council . . . the church questioned herself about her own identity and discovered anew the depth of her mystery as the Body and the Bride of Christ." Considering the Hispanic presence in the American church, we need to question ourselves about the identity of our dioceses and parishes and whether that identity is true to the identities of all the members. We must discover anew in the depth of the mystery of this church, which must be at home with every culture, the many and different gifts that have been given us to share—especially the gift, the blessing, that we are to each other.

It was great news to hear that the CELAM (Episcopal Conference of Latin America), in conjuction with the bishops of North America, has accepted a proposal for a joint synod for the Americas because "we are on the same continent, but so different in origin and history." They have recognized the differences; not only that, they have also realized the energy that can be harnessed precisely from the differences as long as we transcend mere tolerance and move to the level of celebration.

Do we dare celebrate our differences? Have we thought of perhaps a day or a half day for both cultures that includes expressions of prayer and folklore just to celebrate our uniqueness? When we are capable of coming together in celebration, then something positive can happen. Even the preparations for this kind of celebration can be beneficial for opening and advancing reciprocal communication.

There are many challenges ahead of us and still much in each of our two cultures that needs to be discovered, acknowledged and respected with gratitude and responsitility if we are to come together in praise and worship as the one Body of Christ. In the words of John Paul II, "The communion of saints speaks louder than the things that divide us."

Michael S. Driscoll

Liturgy and Devotions: Back to the Future?

If "full, conscious and active participation" in the liturgy is restored to the faithful, will all their spiritual needs be adequately met and extra-liturgical or devotional activity diminish? Thirty years after Vatican II we are seeing a resurgence of devotions in the church.[1] Are devotions really coming back?

A brief glance at many diocesan newspapers in the United States seems to indicate this tendency — everything from novenas to May crownings. Is a return to devotions necessarily retrograde? In the future, will we return to earlier forms of spiritual practices? The question that needs to be addressed is whether devotions are necessarily antithetical to the liturgy or can be complementary to the official forms of worship. This paper will review official attitudes of the church from the Second Vatican Council to the present and explore through the lens of the human sciences why devotions seem to be an essential part of the human faith response.

Toward a Definition of Devotions

So, then, what are devotions? Rather, what is "devotion" and what are "devotions"? "Devotion" is an attitude, a feeling, an affect, while "devotions" represents a multifaceted phenomenon. Definitions from recent theological dictionaries and encyclopedias speak about devotions as distinct from the liturgy, emphasizing their more popular nature:

1. Devotions: non-liturgical prayer forms that promote affective (and sometimes individualistic) attitudes of faith. They may also suggest a more effective response to personal religious needs than liturgical prayer. . . . Devotions might best be understood as a form of popular religion or of personal piety. Popular religion is a bridge between, on the one hand, the more formal celebrations and the intellectual teaching of the faith and, on the other, the appropriation and expression of that faith in the ordinary culture of a particular historical period.[2]

2. Devotion is the feeling side of Christian faith. It consists of emotions and affections which are common and appropriate responses to commitment to Jesus Christ and belief in his gospel within the church. Some components of Christian devotion are admiration at God's wonderful works, a feeling of familiarity with Jesus, abiding sorrow for sin, a sense of security because of God's providential care, the consequent habit of frequently praying about important events in one's life, and joy in companionship with other believers in the church.[3]

3. It is common in academic circles, among historians, medievalists, and students of religion, to employ terms like *popular piety, popular religion,* or *popular devotion.* The qualifier *popular* implies a distinction that is often left implicit. The implied contrast is made explicit in the French dichotomy: *"foi savante, foi populaire,"* referring to a learned or sophisticated faith versus popular belief.[4]

By the time the *Notre Dame Study of Catholic Life* was conducted in the 1980s, devotions were well on the decline. Many American Catholics considered devotions "outmoded relics from the church's past."[5] Without determining the future shapes of devotions, the study made clear that there has been a significant shift in Catholic devotional patterns since Vatican II.

On a more sympathetic note, Andrew Greeley champions the cause of devotional life in the church,[6] while Segunda Galilea argues that the common term "popular religiosity" should be replaced with the theologically richer "popular spirituality," where spirituality means "the practices and attitudes which express the experience of God in a person, a culture, a Christian community."[7]

Perhaps at this time at our juncture in our history, it is time to take a fresh look at devotions, seeing them not as antithetical to liturgy but inspired by, complementing and leading back to the official worship of the church. So we affirm, as Zawilla does, that "[i]f devotion is the desire to respond to God with gratitude for God's gift of faith, and devotions are concrete expressions of that desire, then the best way to critique them is to consider them in relationship to the liturgy."[8]

Official Attitudes toward Devotions

Vatican II

The Second Vatican Council dealt in the first session with the reform of the liturgy. Several paragraphs were dedicated to devotions, especially to their right and wrong use. The Council fathers, in declaring that the liturgy is the "source and summit" of the church's life (SC, 10), nevertheless were careful to establish parameters around the full benefits of the church's liturgical life:

> The sacred liturgy does not exhaust the entire activity of the church. Before men [sic] can come to the liturgy they must be called to faith and to conversion. . . . To believers also the church must ever preach faith and penance; she must prepare them for the sacraments, teach them to observe all that Christ has commanded, and encourage them to engage in all the works of charity, piety and the apostolate, thus making it clear that Christ's faithful, though not of the world, are to be the lights of the world and are to glorify the Father before men (SC, 9).

Balthasar Fischer, in revisiting the question of devotions, laments the "regrettable monopoly of the eucharistic celebration."[9] Looking to the preconciliar period when the eucharist on Sundays and feasts by necessity had to be celebrated in the morning, he notes that the afternoon vespers provided an alternative occasion to pray that nourished the eucharistic celebration. While affirming the central importance of the eucharist as the "summit" of the church's life of prayer and worship, he rightfully notes that for the eucharist to be the summit, it presumes a relationship to other forms of prayer. That which exists all alone cannot be a summit. Therefore Fischer advocates other forms of prayer, liturgical, para-liturgical and devotional, which will serve to complement the eucharistic liturgy.

Fischer makes a critique of the American scene since the Council from the perspective of the liturgical movement and the disappearance of devotions on the one hand, and the concern of the American bishops regarding the lacuna of devotions on the other. "The idea according to which the faithful would live only with the official liturgy henceforth celebrated in their language and understood—liturgy in the conciliar sense of the term—appears clearly as utopian. In the long run, in the lacuna thus created a form of uncontrolled and uncontrollable emotion would spread."[10]

The *Constitution on the Sacred Liturgy* recognizes the limits of liturgy to satisfy all the spiritual demands of the faithful, and it established norms as to how devotions might contribute back to the liturgical life of the church.[11] Paragraph 13 is critical for the discussion of devotions:

> Popular devotions of the Christian people, provided they conform to the laws and norms of the church, are to be highly recommended, especially where they are ordered by the Apostolic See. Devotions proper to individual churches also have a special dignity if they are undertaken by order of the bishops according to customs or books lawfully approved. But such devotions should be drawn up that they harmonize with the liturgical seasons, accord with the sacred liturgy, are in some way derived from it, and lead the people to it, since in fact the liturgy by its very nature is far superior to any of them. (SC, 13)

While the *Constitution on the Sacred Liturgy* calls for the critique of popular devotions using the official liturgy as a norm, it recognizes and endorses the existence of popular rites. This will be important, especially if the liturgy is to be fully inculturated into any particular culture. It is often the devotional dimension which lends itself to cultural adaptation.[12]

The expression "popular religion" and its parallels do not appear in the documents of Vatican II; only the word "popular" appears in regard to religious singing in the liturgy.[13] A number of the documents, nonetheless, seem to make oblique reference to the phenomenon without using the technical terms.[14] Nevertheless, the bishops understood that devotional practices constituted one area where reforms should begin. The church's pastoral attitude to popular devotions would indicate that the intention of the Council was not to suppress devotions but rather to bring them in line with official church liturgy. In upholding the *legitimacy of plurality* in the church, the Council endorsed the enrichment of the church through cultural heritage (cf. LG, 13). Each people expresses itself through ethnicity, customs and the particular genius of the group collectively and individually. Just as individuals within these communities offer their special gifts to further the mission of the church, so too the collectivity offers its unique gifts. The catholicity of the church, therefore, fosters legitimate diversity, inherent to the praise of God.

The question immediately arises: Who is able to determine legitimate diversity? Who within the ethnic and local community decides concerning the preservation and reform of all lawfully recognized rites? Marina Herrera makes the valid point that only those who are within the various ethnic communities will be able to read the symbolic meanings within the cultural manifestation of devotion and liturgy, and they must necessarily be involved in the reform of their devotional life, which is linked to the traditional cultures and is linguistically bound to it.[15]

Postconciliar Developments

The Council mandated that popular devotions conform to the norms of the church itself and harmonize with the liturgical seasons and practices. In fact, popular devotions should flow from the

Michael S. Driscoll

liturgy and return to it. This goal was noble but not always attainable, as Paul VI noted some years later during the Holy Year of 1975:

> Popular religiosity of course certainly has its limits. It is often subject to penetration by many distortions of religion and even superstition. It frequently remains at the level of forms of worship not involving a true acceptance by faith. It can even lead to the creation of sects and endangers the true ecclesial community. But if it is well oriented, above all by a pedagogy of evangelization, it is rich in values. It manifests a thirst for God which only the simple and the poor can know. It makes people capable of generosity and sacrifice even to the point of heroism. . . . [I]t involves an acute awareness of profound attributes of God . . . (and) it engenders interior attitudes rarely observed to the same degree elsewhere.[16]

Two tendencies emerged in the pastoral practice after Vatican II that contradicted the intentions of the council on the question of devotions. On the one extreme, there were those who completely suppressed popular devotions, creating a vacuum. On the other extreme, there were those who created a hybrid sort of liturgy mixing official liturgy and devotions in unequal parts. Often, in the latter case, the liturgy is subordinated to popular devotion.[17] Paul VI remained firm in his conviction about the importance of liturgy, but he did not see popular devotions as antithetical to the liturgy.[18]

In convening the Synod on Evangelization, Paul VI was particularly interested in the sacramental and liturgical life of the church as a privileged place for the renewal of popular faith. The "red" (or preparatory) document for the Synod on Evangelization addressed the relationship of popular piety to liturgy: "An important aid will be given, for the renewal of popular faith, through catechesis and a truly meaningful liturgy, capable of interpreting and transforming life, showing God as accessible in the concrete situations of life" (DR, 132). Nevertheless, popular devotions had the tendency to become "a substitute for a liturgy too distant from the comprehension and from the expressions of the faithful."[19] Rather than being antithetical to the liturgy, popular devotions should become a springboard for the liturgy. Using the principles of inculturation, the liturgy could be prudently adapted to situations or particular groups, thereby fostering growth and a deepening of faith.[20]

In subsequent years the theme of the relationship between devotions and liturgy would be taken up by regional episcopal conferences, especially in Latin America. When the Latin American bishops met for the third time at Puebla in 1979, they were particularly interested in ways to inculturate the gospel so that the Good News might be intelligible and applicable in Third World settings:

> At its core the piety of the people is a storehouse of values that offers answers of Christian wisdom to the great questions of life. The Catholic wisdom of the people is capable of fashioning a vital synthesis. . . . It creatively combines the divine and the human, Christ and Mary, spirit and body, communion and institution, person and community, faith and homeland, intelligence and emotion. This wisdom is a Christian humanism that radically affirms the dignity of every person as a child of God, inserted into a basic fraternity, teaches people to encounter nature and understand work, provides reasons for joy and humor even in the midst of a very hard life. For the people, this wisdom is also a principle of discernment and an evangelical instinct through which they spontaneously sense when the gospel is served in the church and when it is emptied of its content and stifled by other interests.[21]

Far from regarding popular piety as a hindrance to the task of evangelization, the Latin American bishops focused on the positive aspects, such as "a sense of the sacred and the transcendent; openness to the Word of God; marked Marian devotion; an attitude for prayer; a sense of friendship, charity and family unity; an ability to suffer and to atone; Christian resignation in irremediable situations; and detachment from the material world."[22] Nevertheless, these same bishops looked soberly at some of the negative aspects that unbridled popular piety might represent, such as a lack of a sense of belonging to the church; a divorce between faith and real life; a disinclination to receive the sacraments; an exaggerated estimation of devotion to the saints, to the detriment of knowing Jesus Christ and his mystery; a distorted idea of God; a utilitarian view of certain forms of piety; an inclination, in some places, toward religious syncretism; the infiltration of spiritism, and in some areas, of Oriental religious practices.[23]

While admitting to the positive potential of popular piety, the Latin American bishops recognized that devotions are subject to deformations. Remaining at the level of mere cultural manifestations, popular piety can lead to the formation of sects. Nevertheless, the values in popular piety outweigh the dangers, helping to satisfy people's spiritual needs, leading them to be generous and to finding a profound sense of God's loving presence. Popular piety could be an important tool in developing a sense of interiority.

If Paul VI raised the question about the positive value of popular piety, John Paul II seems to have answered affirmatively. Through his trips and his addresses, the current pontiff takes particular care to empower and deepen popular religiosity. Three convictions seem to motivate his words and actions: confidence in popular piety; the conviction that the church, the People of God, is not limited to an elite; and the putting into action of this piety as a way to evangelization.[24]

In 1982, John Paul II, speaking to the French bishops in the Provence–Mediterranean region, underlined the complementarity of the terms "popular religion," "popular Christianity," "popular faith" and "popular piety." All these expressions have the advantage of characterizing "a faith rooted deeply in a precise culture, tied to the fibers of the heart as much as to ideas, and above all widely shared by an entire people, who are the People of God."[25]

Shortly thereafter, John Paul II's conviction about the good use of popular piety found its way into the final synthesis report of the extraordinary Synod of 1985. In looking at the Latin American episcopal conference at Medellin (1968) and the *Evangelii nuntiandi* (1975) of Paul VI, he recommended that pastors give greater attention to popular devotions so that these may be properly understood and correctly practiced. John Paul II refuses to restrict popular piety to a vague feeling without solid doctrinal foundations, thus reducing it to an inferior form of religious manifestation. Further, he affirms the relationship between religiosity and liturgical life based upon the central belief of Christianity, namely, the Incarnation of God in history. Christianity by its nature is an incarnated religion deeply rooted in culture and in different ethnic groups, and must be profoundly lived and rooted in the people.[26]

During the papal visits to Peru and Paraguay, John Paul II gave much attention to the connection between "the proclamation of Jesus Christ" and "the celebration of his mystery in the liturgy of the church." But to the degree that "the liturgy is essentially a work of the church . . . it should be the mirror of the ecclesial community": In his view, popular religiosity appropriately directed is, par excellence, the mold from which it is possible to "prolong the encounter with the mystery of Christ" (3). In his speech to the bishops of Peru, he dealt exclusively with the theme of popular religiosity. While the Pope encourages the participation of the faithful in the sacramental life (eucharist, penance, anointing of the sick), popular devotions are regarded as complementary to these sacraments.

If the documents of Vatican II are remarkably silent about popular piety, the new *Catechism of the Catholic Church* makes explicit those ideas contained in Vatican II in light of postconciliar developments. Three articles (#1674–1676) especially deal with the relationship of piety to the liturgical and sacramental life of the church:

> 1674 Besides sacramental liturgy and sacramentals, catechesis must take into account the forms of piety and popular devotions among the faithful. The religious sense of the Christian people has always found expression in various forms of piety surrounding the church's sacramental life, such as the veneration of relics, visits to sanctuaries, pilgrimages, processions, the stations of the cross, religious dances, the rosary, medals, etc.

> 1675 These expressions of piety *extend* the liturgical life of the church but do *not* replace it. They ["should be so drawn up that they *harmonize* with the liturgical seasons, *accord* with the sacred liturgy, are in some way *derived* from it and *lead the people to it,* since in fact the liturgy by its very nature is far superior to any of them"]. *(SC, 13, 3)*

Michael S. Driscoll

1676 Pastoral discernment is needed to sustain and support popular piety and, if necessary, to purify and correct the religious sense which underlines these devotions so that the faithful may advance in knowledge of the mystery of Christ. Their exercise is subject to the care and judgment of the bishops and to the general norms of the church.

The Human Sciences

If, as these church documents hold, popular piety is so deeply encoded in human experience and in the need for extra-liturgical ways to express religious sentiment and prayer, then let us turn our attention to the human sciences to ask why these devotional forms are so encoded. Admittedly, while moving out of a defined discipline into new areas of inquiry brings some unease, one must, nevertheless, avow that historical and liturgical analysis alone has rendered inconclusive results. The purpose of this exploration, therefore, is to look to the human sciences for alternative ways of explaining the phenomenon of popular piety. Dimensions for further inquiry include the psychological, sociological, cultural and anthropological aspects. Just as liturgical study in recent years has looked to ritual studies to explain how rituals work, other areas of human sciences may bring alternative ways of explaining *why* and *how* devotions work. If, as noted above, devotions spring from human nature, then theologians cannot make an exclusive claim for their study. The human sciences have the advantage of "contextualizing devotions within the larger movements and concerns of a particular culture and age."[27] Rather than a definitive response to the question of devotions, these three areas are proposed for future development: psychology, sociology and cultural anthropology.

Psychology

Devotional activity may be so deeply entrenched because believers cannot find spiritual or emotional sustenance in the liturgy alone.

In 1975, Carl Dehne sketched out several characteristics of devotions.[28] His list indicates how many of these characteristics are of a psychological order. Feelings and familiarity play an important part in the development of spiritual life. Popular piety accentuates the affective dimension of prayer and provides familiarity because the forms are repeated. These often repeated forms allow people to develop a sense of interiority. A similar kind of phenomenon can be noted in the music coming from the communities at Taizé and Iona. By using canons and repeating musical formulas *(ostinati),* the affective dimension is further developed.

One frequent criticism of the reformed liturgy is the lack of time for private prayer and the lack of quiet. Nevertheless, when devotional prayer is exaggerated, it assumes an unhealthy place in the life of the church. Exaggerated devotional activity overshadows the liturgy and places the official prayer of the church at risk. Why then are some people more committed to popular devotions than to the public worship of the church? Patrick Malloy poignantly asks:

> Are Catholics relying so strongly on "popular religion" because the "official religion" fails to respond to their genuine and wholesome needs? If so, how, in light of these questions, can pastoral liturgists minister more effectively? Approaching the question from this angle, liturgists can see the devotional revival, not as a threat, but as an opportunity for ministerial renewal."[29]

Maybe those who favor devotions should not be seen as enemies of the liturgy but as valuable critics.

How often have we heard the complaint that the reformed liturgy has lost a sense of mystery? When liturgists take people's complaints more seriously, will there be less of a tendency to impose "good liturgy" on people based upon theories and ideologies that have very little to do with how people actually pray? As Malloy states, "If the liturgy is truly the 'work of the people,' then the people must be the liturgist's first concern."[30] The psychological approach can provide much in the way of determining people's affective needs in prayer and in finding ways in which the liturgy might better meet that along with devotions.

Michael S. Driscoll

Sociology

A sociological analysis, among other things, can help explain how religion works in society and in the process of social identification. On the American scene, sociologists of religion analyze the upward movement of immigrant groups through the generations. Sociological analysis may provide us with ways of determining how religious practices aid in the movement of immigrants into the mainstream of American society.

According to Harry Stout, most religions in the United States follow a similar three-stage development. In the first stage, the religion of the immigrant is inextricably bound to ethnic identity. Germans, for example, were expected to be either Lutheran or Catholic, whereas Irish and Italian immigrants were assumed to be exclusively Catholic. The self-identification is both ethnic and religious. In the second stage, there is a breaking down of the immigrant religions into Protestant or Catholic or Jewish or Black ethno-religions. Lutherans of German or Swedish ancestry, to give one example, identify themselves less as "German" or "Swedish" and more as "Lutheran" or simply "Protestant." In the third stage, civil religion is attained, whereby one extols the American way of life itself, characterized by individual pragmatism and materialism. At this final stage, assimilation is so complete that neither ethnic identity nor denomination are strong identifiers.[31]

It is worthwhile to note that while the nineteenth-century immigrants have been for the most part assimilated into the American way of life, there are now new waves of immigrants represented ostensibly by Spanish speakers. This phenomenon presents a new paradigm, where American Catholics are both at the center and at the periphery of society. Religious identity will function differently for those who have been assimilated than for those recently arrived. Different criteria must be used for those who have been mainstreamed versus those who are recent immigrants.

Wade Clark Roof observes that after Vatican II, Catholicism moved quickly into the mainstream of American religious life. Prior to the 60s, it had been more concerned with the welfare of its own immigrants members than with shaping the national society. Civil rights activity and the protest against the Vietnam War brought

Catholics into increased cooperation with Protestants and Jews. As mainline Protestantism was losing its place as a dominant voice, the Catholic church moved toward the center. Then in the 1980s, the American bishops emerged as a kind of collective conscience for the nation. They were "activists" seeking to address great issues facing the nation and world at a time when the mood of the country had grown conservative.[32]

Survey findings indicate that the complexion of Catholicism in the United States has been changing, especially as Catholics have become mainstreamed. Along with a higher-educated majority, U.S. Catholics are more diverse in religious interpretations, more at ease in differing with official positions. Decisions of private conscience do not seem to put them at odds with church loyalty. Generally, they remain confident and devout. In the past, the image of American Catholics was of a homogeneous group with uniform religious views and practices. There was little room for dissenters. Now, an attitude of loyal dissent is more prevalent. According to George Cornell, dissenters "are staying explicitly in it [i.e. the church], comfortable in doing so, dedicated to the faith, even though often disagreeing with authorities about its implications;"[33] others are moving into non-Catholic churches. Within American Catholicism today, voluntarism (the choice to remain in the Catholic church or to change denominations) is very apparent. Sociological studies have tracked the spiritual peregrinations of "baby boomers" away from and back toward conventional religion, including many syncretistic alternatives.[34]

Against this ever-changing religious backdrop of American society we must situate the question of devotions: Why would immigrant groups who have been assimilated into the mainstream of society be interested in popular devotions? Would they not be interested in leaving spiritual practices associated with the old world behind in order to blend in better? One possible reason for the reclaiming of old-time religious devotions is precisely for greater ethnic, cultural and religious identification. As people sense a drastic loss of ethnic identity, devotions serve to rekindle ethnicity. Notice, for example, the revival of regional and local ethnic festivals.[35] It may be that *retrieval* is a better word than *revival* to describe what is happening in terms of ethnic, cultural and religious identification. Revival connotes an active moving of the spirit. Revivals and awakenings in our nation's history were synonymous. They connote individual conversion and rededication.[36] But, in a pluralistic society, where an individual's or a group's identity is at stake, the desire to retrieve what was lost, namely identity, becomes an issue. Rather than the official church curtailing or controlling popular religious rites, these rites need to be seen as mediating the community's public horizon and establishing identities within a pluralistic society.[37]

Cultural Anthropology

The sociological paradigm that lumps all Catholics together as though they all arrived in the United States at the same time is no longer tenable. The notions of Roof and McKenney seem to be true for those immigrants who came in the nineteenth and early twentieth centuries. It is true that these immigrants, for the most part, have been successfully mainstreamed. But they are not the entire Catholic church in America. The constant stream of Spanish-speaking immigrants as well as other groups — such as Koreans, Vietnamese and other Asian groups — must also be taken into consideration. The American Catholic church is at the same time at the center and at the periphery of society. What we say about some ethnic groups may not be true for others. What is the relationship of popular religion for those who are still on the margins of the society which they attempt to enter? What is the relationship of religion, especially popular religion, to culture?

Religion stands as one of the primary objects of study by cultural anthropologists who are interested in symbolism, a constitutive dimension of religion. In the study of primitive civilizations, objects under consideration include amulets, totems and rituals. Mythologies of ancient civilizations help to decipher the meaning of the symbolism, much like religious objects and relics aid in understanding the medieval church. Sacred rites are used to define and identify individuals and groups, their relationship to nature, and their collective loyalties and destinies. Since symbolism is constitutive of culture, religion plays an important cultural dimension.

Within this cultural consideration it is appropriate to examine the ritual forms coming from the Hispanic community.[38]

Hispanic ritual forms are an especially rich area of study, especially to the extent that cultural forms are integrated into the official liturgy. Anscar Chapungco, in studying liturgical incultura-tion, states: "Adaptation to various cultures has been a constant feature of Christian liturgy. Indeed, it is part and parcel of her tra-dition, the apostles did it, and so did the Fathers of the church and her pastors far into the Middle Ages. Adaptation of the liturgy to various native genius and tradition is not a novelty but fidelity to tradition."[39] Three ritual forms for consideration are the rites of *posadas* (attached to vespers), *quince años* (a rite of passage which builds on baptismal spirituality) and *novenario* (consisting of the rosary, litanies and vespers).[40] These rites are especially rich for consideration because they have been incorporated into the liturgy or complement it, and they reflect the cultural values of the Spanish-speaking community.

The Hispanic culture is deeply steeped in tradition, and this is reflected in the worship life of the community. In the interest of inculturation, certain ethnic traditions are blended with the offi-cial liturgy of the Catholic church, which respects both the official liturgical forms and the cultural traditions of the Hispanic people. To forge an authentic Hispanic form of worship requires more than uncritically mixing in equal parts some preset ritual form with local customs. According to Arturo Pérez, who has studied these Hispanic ritual forms, "The process is much more complex than that and requires serious study, extensive experimentation and criti-cal evaluation."[41]

The *posadas* celebrations represent a wonderful expression of Hispanic piety. During Advent, two people dressed as Mary and Joseph go symbolically from door to door in search of shelter. At each instance they are turned away, until finally the community lets them in. The celebration can be incorporated with more traditional forms of evening prayer. What is attempted in such a representation is to bring home the coming of Christ to each person individually and collectively. At another level, this ritual reflects the sentiments of Hispanic Americans as they come face-to-face with the Anglo community, the dominant culture which does not always appreciate the Hispanic presence. In the *posadas* the rejection of the Holy Family is a symbol of their experience of rejection. This expression of popular spirituality is based more "on creating an ambiance of warmth and welcome rather than executing a rite precisely."[42]

The resistance of the Hispanic community to becoming mainstreamed into American society runs contrary to what we have seen with the German, Irish and Italian immigrants, who shifted from greater ethnic identity to more homogenized denominational identity. The goal of former immigrants, was to be "Americanized."[43] This is not true of Mexican Americans, who resist assimilation. What is different about Mexican Americans is that they did not immigrate as much as they were conquered. The problems of persistent poverty have not allowed them to ascend to the middle class. They resist the powerful dynamic of assimilation, and their rituals can be an effective way of embodying their resistance.

Conclusion

Some questions still remain concerning devotions and their appropriate use. Are all devotions backward-looking? Are we going back to the future? While some devotions may appear to be retrograde, other forms need not be, especially if they are inspired by the liturgy and return to the liturgy. Leonard Boyle has studied the question from the angle of medieval piety, offering a more nuanced perspective. His first assertion is that both liturgy and devotions flow from faith. He resists the French distinction between *foi savante* and *foi populaire*, stating that both devotions and liturgy are "of the people" and necessarily popular. Most of the definitions concerning popular piety have set up an antinomy between liturgy and devotions, thus creating a false dichotomy. He proposes four categories which describe the relationships that exist between liturgy and devotions, allowing for varying degrees of affinity.

First, there are forms which are liturgical, properly speaking. This includes everything that belongs to the liturgy itself. Any of the official rites of the church are liturgical, in the strict sense of the word.

Second, there are semi-liturgical forms. These are devotions directly inspired by the liturgy. Vespers, for example, is an official liturgical form which lends itself to devotional adaptation and application. When this prayer moves far enough away from the official liturgical form, we might say that it is "semi-liturgical."

Third, "para-liturgical" forms include devotions that are not related to the liturgy but are not antithetical to liturgy. An example of this form would be any type of prayer that may be inspired by a liturgical feast or season. The lighting of the Advent wreath accompanied by prayer, for example, certainly flows from the liturgy and returns to the liturgy, but it is not liturgical *per se*.

Lastly, there are truly anti-liturgical forms, which are those devotions that run counter to the liturgy.[44] In this last category are many types of popular devotion too numerous to mention here.

This categorization permits the evaluation of certain forms of popular piety in terms of the degree of complementarity with the liturgy. Furthermore, Leonard Boyle recognizes that it is the same faith which expresses itself in and through the liturgy and which may seek expression alongside the liturgy. Any historical treatment of devotions indicates their timeliness. Devotions come and go in the history of the church, arising in particular times and in particular places because of particular needs. But because the liturgy is normative and universal in the worship life of the church, the authenticity of devotional forms can and must be judged by the relationship of the devotions to the liturgy.[45]

In the end, one must decide by which criteria devotions should be evaluated. Marina Herrera proposes five questions to help in this process:[46]

1. Do devotions respect the centrality of the person?[47]

2. Do devotions bring about a deeper awareness of religious feelings and interiority of the poor and less educated members of church?

Michael S. Driscoll

3. Do devotions adequately represent the needs and sensibilities of the people who use them, and are they theologically appropriate? It is clear that pastors, in addition to having theological acumen, must have deep knowledge of their people.

4. Is this pastoral knowledge accompanied by respect and appreciation for the unique contribution of those with simple faith?

5. Have the criteria for evaluation of popular devotions been established from within the local practicing community?

While admitting the importance of sensitive outside experts, only those from within the culture itself can evaluate the cultural resonance of certain ritual and spiritual forms. The final judgment is reached only when there is assurance that the meaning of the phenomenon for those involved has been thoroughly understood.

If devotions are to respect the official norms of the church as put forth at Vatican II and more recently, they should be sensitive to three areas, namely: holistic spirituality, liturgical renewal and ecumenical concern.

First, devotions can be helpful for spiritual growth if they promote affective wholeness. Since affectivity is a necessary component of authentic liturgical participation, devotions should not compete with the liturgy but must necessarily be complementary. To this end, the resurgence of devotions does not signal a failure of the liturgical movement but marks the perimeters of liturgy.[48] Devotions in this sense complete that which the liturgy cannot always do, namely promote an affective response. But if devotions seem to fracture the human person so that the spiritual dimension is subordinated or not able to be integrated with other dimensions of life, then devotions are not helpful.

A second sensitivity flows from the first: To be helpful, devotions must promote genuine liturgical renewal in the church and in individuals. In order that devotions might be complementary to liturgy, they must be modeled on an approach which is integrated to the post-conciliar liturgies. To this end, liturgists themselves need to get more involved in the shaping of devotions, tending to such areas as inculturation and liturgical appropriateness. An example of this is the Good Friday liturgy. As diligent as liturgists have been in promoting the official liturgy, popular forms of devotions, like the stations of the cross, still eclipse the official liturgy. It might be that liturgists need to attend to the reasons for this popularity and use their findings to renew the official liturgy, incorporating into it legitimate expressions of popular spirituality.

Lastly, an impassioned word must be said about ecumenical sensitivity. From a historical perspective, we know that devotions have been a strong divisive element — a kind of *bête noire* — a source of disunity and an ongoing cause inhibiting unity among Christians whether they be Orthodox, Latin Catholics or Reformed churches. One explanation of the strong resistance may be that devotions seem to produce an attitude of "works righteousness." In some devotions, for example, rather than commending oneself to God's providence, one takes certain initiatives. Devotions to Mary or the communion of saints could fit into this category. Nonetheless, there are legitimate ways to pray devotionally which can avoid this risk and which can also foster Christian unity. Marian piety that is scripturally based would not only be ecumenically sensitive but spiritually sound.

At the beginning of this essay, we asked whether devotions are retrograde. To this question we reply that they need not be. In fact, to the extent that devotions can emerge with new religious symbols and reinterpret old ones, they will be meaningful and authentic. In their proper context and good use, devotions can be a means of connecting the past with the present in order to face the future.[49] The necessity still remains of forging authentic devotional forms which will be expressive of contemporary and inculturated religious identity. Within American society, the search for identity continues. If devotions can be forged that will speak to the people of a new generation, then they will reflect the genius of the American culture and further the mission of the American church.[50]

1. In *The Wall Street Journal* we read: "The image of the Virgin Mary has appeared to true believers in many places over the years, from a nursing-home window in Rochester, N.Y., to a Chinese elm in North Hollywood, Calif., to a dirty kitchen window in Oxnard, Calif. Now, in the tiny south Texan town of Elsa, she is making a personal appearance on the driver's side rear fender of Dario Mendoza's 1981 maroon Chevrolet Camaro," *The Wall Street Journal* 29 (September 1993): section B, page 1.

Michael S. Driscoll

2. R. Duffy, "Devotions," in *Encyclopedia of Catholicism,* ed. R. McBrien (San Francisco: Harper Collins, 1995): 414.

3. Carl Dehne, SJ, "Devotion and Devotions," in *The New Dictionary of Theology,* eds. J. Komonchak, M. Collins and D. Lane (Wilmington: Michael Glazier, 1989): 283.

4. Ronald Zawilla, "Popular Devotions," in *The New Dictionary of Catholic Spirituality,* ed. M. Downey (Collegeville: Michael Glazier, 1993): 271.

5. Jim Castelli and Joseph Gremillion, *The Emerging Parish: The Notre Dame Study of Catholic Life since Vatican II* (San Francisco: Harper, Row & Collins, 1987): 144–145. See especially chapter 8, "Devotions Past and Present."

6. Andrew Greeley, "Theology and Sociology: Validating David Tracy," in *Sociology and Religion: A Collection of Readings* (San Francisco: Harper Collins, 1995): 440. "I am suspicious of the use of the term 'piety' to describe religious sensibility or subculture. 'Piety' seems to imply a person making the stations of the cross or fingering the rosary beads (both unobjectionable behaviors) with little religious sophistication. I also object to the use of the adjective 'popular,' which seems to imply inferior. Therefore I strongly object to the use of the dismissive term 'popular piety' to describe a religious sensibility or subculture. In fact, a religious sensibility in both individual and community can be a sophisticated narrative system with a subtle blend of the experiential and the reflective. One does not begin to learn how to respect such a system by using a demeaning terminology to describe it. All that can be said about the religious sensibility of ordinary people is that it is not the same as that of academic theologians."

7. Segunda Galilea, *Religiosidad Popular y Pastoral Hispano–Americana* (New York: Northeast Catholic Pastoral Center for Hispanics, 1981): 49.

8. Zawilla, ibid.: "In the liturgy of the church, worship is given to God in the spirit of Jesus. There is something universal, something objective, something timeless about the liturgy, above all the eucharist. The eucharist realizes in ritual form the response of Jesus to God. It is, from the standpoint of Christian faith, the most perfect sacrifice of praise and thanks that can be offered to God. As the summit of Christian worship, it is the reference point of the other sacraments and the Liturgy of the Hours, which lead to or flow from the Eucharist."

9. Balthasar Fischer, "Relation entre liturgie et piété populaire après Vatican II: la réception de l'article 13 de *Sacrosanctum Concilium,*" *La Maison Dieu* 170 (1987): 96.

10. Ibid.: 98. See also Hans Bernard Meyer, SJ, who studied the couplet liturgy/popular piety. Everything that is liturgy is *pia* or *sacra exercitia,* while all that is popular piety is everything that belongs to the domain of extracultual or popular religiosity.

11. *Sacrosanctum Concilium,* in *Documents of Vatican II,* ed. A. Flannery (Grand Rapids: William B. Eerdmans Publishing, 1984): "The spiritual life, however, is not limited solely to participation in the liturgy. The Christian is indeed called to pray with others, but he must also enter into his bedroom to pray to his Father in secret; furthermore, according to the teaching of the apostle, he must pray without ceasing. We also learn from the same apostle that we must always carry around in our bodies the dying of Jesus, so that the life also of Jesus may be made manifest in our mortal Flesh. That is why we beg the Lord in the Sacrifice of the Mass that 'receiving the offering of the Spiritual Victim' he may fashion us for himself 'as an eternal gift' (SC, 12).

12. Cf. Timothy Matovina, "Liturgy, Popular Rites, and Popular Spirituality" *Worship* 63 (July 1989): 360.

13. Cf. Albert Verwilghen, SDB, "La religiosité populaire dans les documents récents du Magistère," *Nouvelle Revue Théologique* 109 (July – August 1987): 521.

14. In addition to the *Constitution on the Sacred Liturgy* (*Sacrosanctum Concilium,* [SC]), other conciliar documents include *Lumen gentium* (LG), *Gaudium et spes* (GS), *Nostra Aetate* (NA) and *Ad gentes* (AG).

15. Cf. Marina Herrera, "Popular Devotions and Liturgical Education," *Liturgy* 5:1 (1985): 35. "As liturgical rites are revised, great care is taken to preserve their integrity; so, too, the elimination or change of popular devotions should not be imposed from without, but only by ministers who are familiar with the culture and language of the people they serve."

16. Paul VI, *On Evangelization in the Modern World,* 48 *(Evangelii nuntiandi).*

17. Paul VI notes these two tendencies in his apostolic exhortation *Marialis cultus,* on rightly grounding Marian devotion, February 4, 1974. DOC 3929. Cf. Regis Duffy, "Devotio Futura: The Need for Post-Conciliar Devotions?" in *A Promise of Presence: Studies in Honor of David N. Power, OMI,* ed. M. Downey and R. Fragomeni (Washington, DC.: Pastoral Press, 1992): 165 – 66.

18. "Wise pastoral ministry sets out clearly and explains the inherent nature of liturgical services; it extols and promotes popular devotions in such a way as to adapt them to the needs of individual ecclesial communities and to direct them toward contributing to the liturgy" (*Documents on the Liturgy, 3929* [Collegeville: Liturgical Press, 1982]).

19. Jean Villot, *Lettre pontificale aux commissions liturgiques d'Amérique latine* (July 21, 1977), in *Documentation Catholique* 74 (1977): 911.

20. Cf. Verwilghen, ibid., 534.

21. "Final Documentation of the Third General Conference of the Latin American Episcopacy on the Present and the Future of Evangelization," (Puebla, January 1979): 448; *Construire une civilization de l'amour* (Paris: Centurion, 1980).

22. Ibid., p. 914.

23. Ibid., p. 448.

24. Cf. Verwilghen, Ibid., p. 523.

25. John Paul II, "Allocution to the French bishops of the Provence – Mediterranean Region," *Documentation Catholique* 79 (1982): 1133–1136.

26. Cf. E. Pironio, "Report on the Situation of the Church in Latin America during the Synod on Evangelization," *L'Église des cinq continents. Bilan et perspectives de l'évangélisation* (Paris: Centurion, 1975).

27. Cf. Regis Duffy, "Devotio Futura: The Need for Post-Conciliar Devotions?" in *A Promise of Presence: Studies in Honor of David N. Power, OMI,* ed. M. Downey and R. Fragomeni (Washington, D.C.: Pastoral Press, 1992): 166.

28. Carl Dehne, "Roman Catholic Popular Devotions," *Worship* 49 (1975): 446–460: 1. Popular devotions provide a vehicle through which the worshiper can express personal concerns, religious feelings and deeply held attitudes; 2. They focus on persons, not themes — they are relational; 3. They take the presence of Jesus seriously — eucharistic devotions; 4. They use clear expressions — simple and direct ideas; 5. They tend to move in spirals or circles — conversational; 6. They use ceremonies and symbols — active participation; 7. They are practically invariable — familiarity.

29. Patrick Malloy, "Devotions Revisited" *GIA Quarterly* (Summer, 1994): 12.

30. Ibid., p. 41.

31. Cf. Matovina, Ibid., p. 358; cf. Harry Stout, "Ethnicity: the Vital Center for Religion in America," *Ethnicity* 2 (1975): 204–224.

32. Cf. Wade Clark Roof and William McKenny, *American Mainline Religions: Its Changing Shape and Future* (New Brunswick: Rutgers University Press, 1987): 96.

33. George Cornell, *Religion in America, 1979–80* (Princeton: Princeton Religious Research Center): 75.

34. Cf. R. Stephen Warner, "Work in Progress towards a New Paradigm of Sociology of Religion in the United States," in *American Journal of Sociology* 98 (1993): 1075.

35. Cf. Mary Waters, *Ethnic Option: Choosing Identities in America* (Berkeley: University of California Press, 1990).

36. Cf. Robert Wuthnow, *Rediscovering the Sacred: Perspectives on Religion in Contemporary Society* (Grand Rapids: William B. Eerdmans, 1992): 2–3.

37. Cf. Matovina, ibid., p. 352.

38. So-called "Hispanics" are quick to reply that the term itself is used exclusively within the United States and that it lumps many different ethnic groups together merely on the basis of language. Often the groups under consideration justifiably resist classification in this manner knowing full well that there are worlds of difference between one Spanish-speaking group and another.

39. Anscar Chupungco, *Cultural Adaptation of the Liturgy* (New York: Paulist Press, 1982): 3.

40. Arturo Pérez, *Popular Catholicism: A Hispanic Perspective,* in *American Essays in Liturgy,* 9 (Washington DC: Pastoral Press, 1988): 24. "Such a novena of vespers could effectively combine the official prayer of the church with traditional Hispanic prayer and put both at the service of those who grieve."

41. Ibid., p. 27.

42. Cf. Matovina, Ibid., p. 357.

43. Cf. Jay P. Dolan, *The Immigrant Church* (Notre Dame: Notre Dame Press, 1983).

44. Leonard Boyle, "Popular Piety in the Middle Ages: What is Popular?" *Florilegium* 4 (1982): 184-193.

45. Cf. Zawilla, Ibid., p. 271-72.

46. Cf. Marina Herrera, "Popular Devotions and Liturgical Education," *Liturgy* 5:1 (1985): 36.

47. Ibid., p. 37: "Popular piety can heighten our awareness of the presence of God, the Spirit, the communion of saints, the sacred nature of all life and the full liberation of the total person."

48. Concerning the success of the liturgical renewal, see Philip Murnion, *Parish Life in the United States* (Washington DC: NCCB, 1982): 33. "The intent of Vatican II's reforms, which emphasized intelligibility of the rite and participation of the people, has been remarkably achieved and is being furthered by continuing efforts." Also see the *Notre Dame Study of Catholic Parish Life.*

49. Cf. Virgil Elizondo, "Popular Religion as Support of Identity: A Pastoral Psychological Case-Study Based on the Mexican American Experience in the USA," in *Popular Religion* (Edinburgh: T. & T. Clark, 1986): 42–43.

50. Cf. Regis Duffy, "Devotio Futura: The Need for Post-Conciliar Devotions?" in *A Promise of Presence: Studies in Honor of David N. Power, OMI,* ed. M. Downey and R. Fragomeni (Washington, D.C.: Pastoral Press, 1992): 181.

Thomas F. O'Meara, OP

The Expansion of Ministry:

Yesterday, Today, Tomorrow

In the years after the Second Vatican Council, ministry changed very rapidly. It changed by expanding into areas that before the council hadn't been considered "ministry": education, liturgy and social justice. Ministry changed also by professionalization, for instance in areas such as campus ministry and health care ministry; it changed by a dramatic increase in numbers; it increased in its parish forms and in the development of diocesan offices directing ministry. If we focus on the basic place of ministry, the parish, from 1965 to 1975, we find that parishes changed in terms of which ministries were done and who did them. The parish was no longer a place of rapid Masses in Latin with an occasional baptism or parish dance. The roles of deacons, lectors, cantors and communion bearers illustrated and continue to illustrate the expansion beyond what happens on Sunday mornings.

The early church understood that the liturgical array of ministers existed to nourish the external, evangelistic array of ministers. Now that dual interplay of liturgy and public ministry has returned in directors of different levels of education, ministers involved in worship or social justice, ministers to families, to the aging or to the young, and permanent deacons.

Inevitably, the appearance and activity of the Catholic parish and diocese in North America, and in succeeding years in other parts of the world, changed in this time. For indeed, the very model of ministry changed. Parishes changed in their patterns — theological, ecclesiological and professional — of what was done and who did it.

Reflections on Change

A moment in my life marked by the fissure of the Ecumenical council illustrates this change. I was ordained a priest in the Dominican Order in June 1962, three months before the start of Vatican II. In the summer of 1962, newly ordained Dominicans spent the summer helping out on weekends at parishes in Illinois, Iowa and Wisconsin; the rite we used was that of the Dominican order, a rite that had been in place since the year 1260.

The parish offered Masses and sacraments in Latin and little more. Converts were occasional and quickly instructed; marriages needed brief, mainly legal, preparations; baptisms, except for the gingerly pouring of water, were not intelligible. The non-ordained could not enter the sanctuary (the pre-adolescent altar boys were more angelic than human), and no ministry (that is, no ministry essentially, formally and publicly connected to the church's life as education, liturgy and the RCIA are today) took place outside the sanctuary. Collecting canned goods and coaching basketball are not what Saint Paul had in mind when he used the word *diakonia!*

In short, the parish of 1962 was little different from a parish in 962. In 962 the Norman Vikings were settling down in northern France; it was 300 years before the completion of the cathedral of Notre Dame in Paris and 700 years before the Puritans were founding towns in New England in what would become the United States. The concrete form of the parish of 1962, or of 962, however, does not resemble the parish today in most of the United States, where since 1972 the parish has existed with a post-conciliar experience of ministry.

A second reflection on ministry in transition, past and present, touches the books of the New Testament. In the years just before Vatican II, the American parish was full of repressed vitality; but Sunday morning had little connection with the descriptions of church and ministry which were read at Mass in the letters of the New Testament. What did it mean to say that all Christians were to be active in the Body of Christ when they sat passively facing forward in church pews? What did Paul intend with ideas about a public liturgy of preaching and life and all kinds of services when the activities of the sole minister were silent and isolated, quite disconnected from the many others in the assembly? Why read the lists of ministries in Paul's letters to the Romans and Corinthians when there was only one activity in the church, that of the priest? What did the mention of ministries of "evangelist" or "apostle" mean when no formal outreach in American society took place? The word "ministry" was a Protestant term not used by Catholics, and "charism" was something which tried to make a dangerous figure like Catherine of Siena or Dorothy Day respectable.

But one can easily apply those passages on charisms and ministries to the church we know now and to the churches in which we celebrate. Any parish where the liturgy is done well and where the liturgy is continued in the ministries of education, care and social service does not consist exclusively of a pastor and one or two assistants, with sisters nearby staffing the grade school. The new model involves a staff of full-time ministers, a whole community of ministers, led by the pastor, with their own education, expertise, natural gifts and commission.

The Sources of Change

These changes in ministry, theological and epoch-making, took place from the impetus of the council. Today, the council's documents look rather ordinary, but they set in motion much more than they expressed. Their impetus was such that it has continued and intensified in the years that followed. It is as though the Spirit draws more profound and complex issues out of the conciliar event. The work of Vatican II was to "translate," to "accommodate," to bring up to date (*"aggiornamento,"* as Pope XXIII called it). Was the expansion of ministry a "translation"?

The expansion of ministry was certainly a momentous shift, occurring rapidly and enthusiastically in the United States. This translation, this inculturation, drew on American characteristics: A delight in belonging to groups, a tradition of helping and service, a natural activism. Parish ministry became a celebration of "belonging through active service," an experience typical of American culture and our American way of life.

The impetus for change came from the council's documents: They implied that there was more to be done in a parish than saying a routine Mass or organizing a Halloween dance. When I think back on the preconciliar *parishes* (not other Catholic institutions like schools or hospitals), what I find characteristic of a parish prior to 1965 is indeed how little they did. But the Spirit of the council determined that new theological impetuses would win an influential freedom, a freedom often drawn from venerable traditions and early theologies that had been dormant for some time. The impetuses resulted in significant change in our experience of ministry: They raised up the theology of the people of God over against hierarchy alone; baptism as ordination; grace as empowerment rather than insurance policy; liturgy as the ritual for ministry; a theology of charism flowing into ministry.

At the same time that parishes were expanding their ways of doing liturgy, education and service, society also changed. Its needs and ills became public, and Catholics — no longer suspect in society — could address and meet American society. And, as theology and church were seeking outlets for public action, society offered theology and church countless opportunities.

But change in the form of parish and diocesan offices did not come from bishops, nor from plans drawn up by chancery officials; nor did it come from the methodologies of theologians or from sociological surveys of the Catholic church or from academic observers of American religion. And it certainly did not come about because of a decline in priests. (Although it was not to become evident until the late 1960s, the decline in vocations to the diocesan

Thomas F. O'Meara, op

priesthood and to religious orders of men and women had begun before the council and was likely tied to changes in the aspirations of Catholics, who were no longer of an immigrant world.) The new model of the parish came from the stimulus of Vatican II, and it was providential that this new model was in place to supply ministers during the period of the decline in the number of priests.

Healthy and grand theological movements also come from the grassroots, from dedicated individuals, from changes in activity. Someone sees and lives differently, and others, finding that approach fruitful, get on board. Change is also neither an instant revolution nor a chain of successes.

In old and huge organizations like the Catholic church, change is a complex phenomenon. The past never fully disappears; old forms are not fully replaced; the new must be both incarnational and traditional. If these shifts in church life are considerable and fraught with further implications, their day-to-day realization in the life of the local parish is nevertheless quite ordinary.

Why did this change come about? It is unavoidable to conclude that it came from a deep encounter between the Spirit of the risen Jesus and the people of God. This meeting of Spirit and people, filled with renewal, was prepared for and interpreted by renewed study of the Bible and of the early church. The work of European theologians, whose works recovered and re-emphasized the sacerdotal character of baptism and the dignity of being "a Christian," led to an understanding of Christian life which found that the vocation of being a Christian was much more than being "a layperson" had been before the council. The Holy Spirit was altering and broadening the way the church's members understood themselves and the church's mission. A restored theology of baptism called people to a life whose ministries and charisms were given for the upbuilding of the church. And many communities discovered that there were opportunities for ministry all around.

That theological renewal was put in place, realized and experienced in a particularly expansive way in the American parish. It was a silent change; it began unperceived. I saw its transformation of the Midwest here in the United States and experienced in Nigeria and New Zealand the same dynamics at work. (I wrote my book *Theology of Ministry* not to prescribe a program but to explain what was in fact happening.) Then I learned of base communities, with their ministries, in Latin America. I could only presume that this was happening worldwide.

Yves Congar, Theologian of Ministry

A great change, so great as to be a change in model, had been taking place in the structure of ministry at the local level — parish and diocese, campus and hospital — in the 1960s. But questions emerged: Is this model legitimate? Is this challenge to medieval and Baroque parish patterns permitted? Is it old, or is it new? Is it, perhaps, both old and new at the same time?

Let us pause and look at the post-conciliar reflections on this change in model by the most important ecclesiologist in this century and at Vatican II. In 1994 the great historian and theologian of the church, Yves Congar, was made a cardinal — twenty years late — and not long after died at the age of ninety. Congar was the most influential theologian of Vatican II. The enterprises of his theological career — ecumenism east and west, episcopal collegiality, the theology of the laity, tradition — were the agenda of the council. He could write both researched studies admired by historians and popular essays that would change the way Catholics lived.

At twenty-six he sensed a vocation, a vocation in theology to research the forms of church life in their historical context in order to renew and expand the church. The following years involved meticulous research into the history of offices, laws, rites and theologies of the church. To that was added dozens of talks and sermons on ecumenism, church reformation, the nature of being a bishop or the role of being a layperson. Congar's approach was inspired by the movements going on in France from 1930 to 1960, movements of renewal in scripture, patristic thought and the liturgy, and by the "golden years of Catholic action."[1]

Congar's ecclesiology offered a church that was an organic personal unity of diverse active ministries. He had found this theology in the German Catholic romantic idealist, J.A. Möhler, who in turn had drawn it from Greek patristic thought. In 1953, the French Dominican wrote the first theological system on the laity, *Jalons pour une théologie du laicat* (1953), and *Lay People in the Church* (1957). That book goes far beyond the theologies of the church cultivated in the neo-scholastic period from 1860 to 1950, which Congar described as "a hierarchology."

At the beginning of his book on the laity, Congar wrote:

> It is not just a matter of adding a paragraph or a chapter to an ecclesiological exposition which from beginning to end ignores the principles on which a "laicology" really depends. Without these [new] principles we should have, confronting a laicised world, only a clerical church which would not be the people of God in the fullness of its truth. At bottom there can only be one sound and sufficient theology of laity, and that is a "total ecclesiology."[2]

Twenty years later, after the council, he looked back: "I have not written that ecclesiology."[3]

An essay of 1972, however, did look at his theology of ministry, past and present. It is of interest to us because it mirrors what has happened to ministry since the council. Congar's modesty and honesty let him see his first book's limitations. "I have gradually corrected my vision, which at first was principally and spontaneously clerical."[4] He notes that the framework of priesthood, kingship and prophetic office, as well as the frameworks of the four Aristotelian causes (in Gerard Paris and Charles Journet), must be set aside. Instead, there is a move to an arrangement of charisms and ministries:

> The church of God is not built up solely by the actions of the official presbyteral ministry but by a multitude of diverse modes of service, more or less stable or occasional, more or less spontaneous or recognized, and, when the occasion arises consecrated, while falling short of sacramental ordination. These modes of service do exist. . . . [M]others at home, the person who coordinates liturgical celebrations or reads the sacred text, the woman visiting the sick or prisoners, adult catechists. These are good examples of . . . the church *diakonia*. Such modes of service proceed from gifts of nature or grace, from those callings which Saint Paul names "charisms" since

they are given "for the common good" (1 Corinthians 12:7, 11). They exist right now but up to now were not called by their true name, ministries, nor were their place and status in ecclesiology recognized.[5]

This is very different from the model of a church whose millions, touched by infant baptism and confirmation, share at most in apostolates gingerly bestowed by bishops. The model changed.

Congar wrote: "It is worth noticing that the decisive coupling is not 'priesthood/laity,' as I used it in *Jalons*, but rather 'ministries/modes of community service.'"[6] Congar gave a sketch of the model which would replace the bipolar division of clergy and laity. *It is a circle with Christ and Spirit as ground or animating power upon ministries in community.* He continued: "It would then be necessary to substitute for the linear scheme a scheme where the community appears as the enveloping reality *within which* the ministries, eventually the instituted sacramental ministries, are placed as *modes of service* of what the community is called to be and do."[7] He also speaks of levels of ministry.

One could find a similar ecclesiology in the writings of Karl Rahner. It would begin with the dialogue of each human person with divine grace. That theology of a liturgy of grace, a world of grace, assumes the model of concentric circles. There are degrees of faith and grace arranged around a center which is Christ, the Spirit of God, or the Trinity. Similarly, the parish and diocese today can, from the point of view of ministry, best be understood as a community which has circles of ministries arranged around the pastor or bishop.

Ministry Today and Tomorrow

A great deal happened in the realization of ministry in the 1970s. To prepare in 1970 for a consultation on a national pastoral council (something only slightly realized in an advisory council), I wrote to Yves Congar some questions about ecclesiology. In the conclusion

Thomas F. O'Meara, op

of his answers he wrote: "It is astonishing how the post-conciliar period has so little to do with the Council . . . The post-conciliar questions are new and radical, and *aggiornamento* means changes and adaptations to a new situation, assuming the principles of the original institution."[8]

Finding the format of parish ministry is a work in progress. Changes continue; new ministries dealing with marriage or illness appear; the RCIA has a great impact and often calls forth a separate, well-educated corps interested in ministry. If the new model of ministry has held strong and has expanded, that view of the church as a living, collective personality of social and revealed services has not been formally, ecclesially and structurally sustained in all dioceses.

Within the past few years, I have spoken on ministry at the large parish at Purdue University, at many places in the Archdiocese of Anchorage and at the seminary in Denver. It is clear that the idea of the church as a sacramental fast-food business has been displaced and that the new model of expanded ministry is taken for granted. This has happened because there are so many Catholics, because people want to be involved in ministry and because there is always more to be done if one has the insight, imagination and energy.

So for reasons divine and human, ecclesiological and theological, the new model can only continue for the faithful and their ministers. Unfortunately, while the expansion seems to be the present intention of the Holy Spirit, it is left unanalyzed and unsupported by church policies and practices like the following:

1. There is a lack of planning for what the American church will be in the next century. The growth of the number of Catholics is a problem that is not faced. Some dioceses look ahead in planning for the decline of priests, but the new model is only tolerated, left unexplored or unformalized.

2. Ministry beyond that of the ordained is not taken seriously in terms of incorporation into the diocese and in terms of adequate salary, benefits, appreciation and spiritual life. (This is less true of parishes.) Too many still cling to a weak ecclesiology of "parish workers" who are considered mere replacements for the absent

clergy; they are considered employees without a job. But "ministry" is never a "job." All those serving the presence of the Spirit are bound by a higher calling, a spiritual life.

Cardinal Danneels, primate of Belgium, speaks of the great commission of everyone on the parish team in bearing and forming the community, the work of the Spirit. He singles out human formation, theological and psychological, and then formation in prayer—to which he gives the greatest space.[9] The renewal of ministry from the 1960s to 1990s is the rediscovery of the revolution of the early church: First, the kingdom of God is open to all, and second, its ministrations are incumbent upon all.

3. The needed expansion of ministry and the new model presume financial support. They require greater contributions from Catholics who support other institutions, such as high schools and universities, but who have not been educated in the realism of the financial costs of the new model of parish and diocese.

4. The growth of the Catholic population ensures that the question of ministers cannot be ignored. Through baptism and confirmation, 150,000 adults enter the American church each year: They are potential recipients of education and of a call to ministry. The population of Hispanics in Chicago was expected to increase from 850,000 to 1,100,00 between 1990 and 1995, while sociologists project that the population of American Catholics rose from 60 million to 74 million. While there is great interest in temporary ministry among young Catholics, one must face the end of the church of the nineteenth century. One can expect, for instance, that the withdrawal of 30,000 religious women from active ministry in the next fifteen years can be met only by the expansion of ministry.

5. In some circles of leadership there is the gloomy hope that perhaps ministry, other than what the priest does, will fade away. In this day-dream, full-time ministries of the baptized seem expendable, doomed to exist outside the life of the diocese. In fact, while seminary enrollments have dropped almost 60 percent in three decades, recently, between 1990 and 1993, they fell another 5 percent. (The increase of 20 percent in ordinations between 1990 and

1993 is a minor fluctuation drawn from a small base). Poor retention of young priests after ordination is a further problem. It points to dubious quality. In fact, four out of ten ordained are needed just to replace young priests, and so the other six can barely replace the remaining priests. While the diocesan priesthood will decline by 40 percent between 1996 and 2005, the Catholic population will increase by 65 percent. The idea of a "golden age" and its return is not only historically unlikely but is pastorally inadequate.

An archdiocese like Chicago has over 2000 full-time ministerial positions, and one cannot imagine these all being replaced by a new surge of priestly vocations. Their ministry is not that of the presbyter. The diversity of ministries precludes a return to the medieval and Baroque theology of one minister, a theology which is less rich than those of the first centuries and foreign to the theology that emerged from Vatican II. The priest or pastor remains central, for the leader of the community is a presbyter and not vice-versa. The church certainly needs leaders of the local church — pastors and bishops — but the idea of a sudden shift to anything approaching the number of competent priests is fantasy. Such nostalgia presents poor theology. The presbyter/pastor is not the only minister, although it was such from the eighth century to Vatican II. The role and ministry of the pastor has not been threatened by the diversification of his world of ministries, but in a way he has been set free and given a clearer identity. This is a difficult position, and the pastor is the unsung hero of our post-conciliar period.

6. The consequence of the new model of concentric circles of ministry does not compromise the roles of bishop and pastor, but it does imply that the church can no longer be divided into clerics and laity. Each group in the church, from readers to cardinals, has its own distinctive calling and its own graced life.

The nonordained ministries of the church today are not composed of people who are failed aspirants to the one sacerdotal ministry. There are many gifts and services in the Body of Christ, and they are not in competition with one another. The pastoral administrator illustrates the difficulty of pursuing pastorally the new model of ministry while refusing to accept its theological implications. At the same time, this new ministry serves a positive purpose because it helps people become used to new images and realities of ministry at the local level. The ethos of a ministry which is only "lay," of the temporary church employee, is dangerous because it undermines the Catholic presupposition that ministry and spirituality are joined together. Can the lay minister follow just any lifestyle? There must be demanding Christian lifestyles for all in ministry, ways of living the gospel which are neither solely monastic nor purely secular. We must admit that we do not know what the church would look like at the international level, although we know something of what it looks like at the parish level.

Conclusion

The dynamics of the Second Vatican Council shifted the church's life away from an emphasis upon central organization that lasted 400 years. A re-emphasis of facets of the early church, like wider ministry, will take longer than a few decades. The ministering church must be patient. If we are in the midst of an unprecedented change in parish and diocesan life, of a return to the charismatic revolution of Jesus' followers, we cannot expect history and church to race forward. We have today the first generations of the change — the first generations of lay theologians, religious educators, directors of the RCIA — who are directing the new ministries.

Isn't the hurly-burly, unplanned grassroots evolution of expanded ministry preferable to a liberal church leadership imposing enlightened, even biblical, views on a disinterested constituency? History shows that part of the organic dynamics of the church is an active tension between institutions and charisms, except that now we realize that both every office and every charism is supposed to be both charismatic and ministerial.

In 1960, on the eve of Vatican II, Karl Rahner wrote an essay expressing his hope that the council would do something new. For its title, he chose a line from Saint Paul: "Do not extinguish the Spirit." Rahner's words — and Saint Paul's words — had a great impact on the following years of Vatican II. We all have at work in us, in silence and in each second of time, the baptismal charisms of the Holy Spirit. The Spirit suggests patiently that which would further its plans. As Jesus, Saint Paul, and Thomas Aquinas state, we are the Spirit's students, friends and coworkers.

1. Yves Congar, "My Path-Findings in the Theology of Laity and Ministries," *The Jurist* 2 (1972): 170 – 171. See R. McBrien "Church and Ministry: the Achievement of Yves Congar," *Theology Digest* 32 (1985): 203ff.

2. Yves Congar, *Lay People in the Church* (Baltimore, 1957), p. xvi.

3. Yves Congar, "My Path-Findings in the Theology of Laity and Ministries," *The Jurist* 2 (1972): 169.

4. Ibid., p. 181.

5. Ibid.

6. Ibid., p. 176.

7. Ibid., p. 178.

8. Private letter of 9 December 1970.

9. Danneels in *La Documentation Catholique* (March 5, 1995): 228 – 229.

Theresa F. Koernke, IHM

Eucharist: From Rubricism to Freedom

After the electoral conclave following the death of Pope Pius XII in 1959, the Cardinal Prefect announced that Angelo Giuseppe Roncalli would sit in the Chair of Peter as John XXIII. Because of his advanced age, 77, and poor health, some thought that he would halt the theological movements of the church beyond the apparently orderly, safe world of neoscholastic theology.

It would be an understatement to say that the Holy Spirit surprised us all through Pope John's call to *aggiornamento* by way of an ecumenical council. Indeed, many thought that we would do well to simply reaffirm the material discussed at the First Vatican Council (1869–70). The *De Ecclesia* of Vatican I had asserted that the church was composed of radically unequal persons.

During my student days at Marygrove College of Detroit (1961–66), the curriculum was changed in order to incorporate such documents as the *Dogmatic Constitution on Divine Revelation*, the *Decree on the Renewal of Religious Life*, the *Dogmatic Constitution on the Church*, the *Pastoral Constitution on the Church in the Modern World*, the *Decree on the Apostolate of Lay People*, and *The Constitution on the Sacred Liturgy* (CSL).

Theresa F. Koernke, IHM

Although we did not speak as readily as we do now about the "liturgy of the sacraments" — especially the eucharist — as the lightning rod for almost every issue in the church, the years since the promulgation of the CSL have revealed the celebration of the eucharist to be just that: The place where issues of authority and leadership either collapse or openly clash with the urge of the laity to assume our rightful place in church life. Many of us were bent on breaking out of the Tridentine liturgy, which revolved almost completely — theologically, catechetically and certainly performatively — around what the ministerial priest did. We wanted so much to adapt the liturgy to our culture.

And so, thinking to break the shackles of the rubrics that priests had been bound to observe under pain of sin, we gave ourselves at times to "creativity," which really meant: "Never do anything the same way twice," or "Seldom or never do what the directives say."

On the one hand, there is a sense in which that reaction was understandable, as will be obvious. On the other hand, that reaction did lead to indiscretions, some of which Anscar Chupungco discussed.

What did we think was "all that really matters" at Mass? For centuries, and even though we went through the readings, the theology and catechesis concentrated on what the priest said over the bread and wine. It seems to me that the idea that we could change anything before or after those powerful words was quite understandable. Indeed, those words were thought to be so powerful that some priests used cookies and milk or chips and Coke, and all with the desire to escape the seeming prison of rubrics and to be "relevant."

We put all sorts of things — school books and biology mice, sports equipment and birthday cakes — on the altar table at the preparation of the gifts, wanting so much to have the Mass "be an expression of our lives." Priests passed the sacramentary around for lay folks to read sections of the eucharistic prayer to encourage "participation," or so we thought. And many of our people thought that the priest was so nice to say such things as: "Good morning!

Thank you for being here to pray with me at my Mass. This won't take long."

These and other examples did lead to the reaction of the Congregation for Divine Worship, which in many ways was also understandable. Still, these indiscretions gave a kind of false credibility to those who condemned the reforms of Vatican II in favor of the Liturgy of Trent.

Thirty years after the promulgation of the CSL, we are in a precious position to ask, yet again: What do we think we are doing when we gather for the eucharist? How can we appreciate our various reactions to the conciliar reform? How can we evaluate our current practice in order to move from rubricism to genuine freedom? The following presents a *context* in which we can reflect upon our celebration of the grace, mercy and peace revealed to us in the celebration of the eucharist.

Much has changed in the thirty years since Vatican II. Indeed, our understanding of the world has had an impact on our notion of God, the saving meaning of Christ, the structure of the church and the conceived relationship of human beings to each other and to the cosmos. How have these changes influenced our notions of eucharist, of "the very nature of the liturgy," of "creativity," of rubrics and of inculturation, and most especially of the feminist critique of the liturgy? During these years we have used figures of speech like "progressive" liturgy and "conservative" liturgy. Yet what have we meant? In a quiet moment, I asked: *What if there were no rubrics in our liturgical books? What convictions about the origin and meaning of the eucharist would guide our practice?*

What follows is in four parts: setting the context, a reflection on the influence of cosmology on thought and behavior, consequences of this for the liturgical movement, and celebrating the eucharist: from rubricism to freedom.

Setting the Context: Historical Consciousness

An examination of journals of sociology, anthropology and liturgical studies shows that the topic of *human ritual behavior* has been drawing intense comment.[1] This is not at all surprising, because the ritual patterns of a social group are the locus of communal identity. Obviously, therefore, the repetitive, interpersonal, value-laden behaviors,[2] which we know as the liturgy of the sacraments, are of interest to us as we strive to remember where we have come from so that we might know how to enter into our future as the Body of Christ in history.

There is a truism in the philosophy of knowledge that is pertinent to our reflection on the reception of the liturgical reforms at the time immediately after the Second Vatican Council, and especially at this time in the history of that ongoing reception. That dictum says: *Quidquid recipitur per modum recipientis recipitur.* "Whatever is received, is received according to the mode of the receiver." Put another way, each of us heard or "received" the mandate for reform of the liturgy and for the spiritual renewal that this reform implied, according to a specific view of the world (cosmology) and the more or less conscious view of the relationship of God to the world.

Today, we are paying much attention to this fact through the term "historical consciousness." What is historical consciousness? We have all studied events and persons in the church and in societies. Historical consciousness, however, refers to two aspects in the process of knowing. One aspect refers to our recognition that persons act and events occur within a given social, spiritual and intellectual atmosphere, indeed, that the cosmology of a people and period of time is bound to influence thought and behavior. (Recall the fear that Christopher Columbus would fall off the edge of the earth.) The other related aspect of historical consciousness refers to our recognition that we too are operating out of one cosmology or a combination of cosmologies. Here, historical consciousness refers not simply to knowledge about events and persons but to the awareness or consciousness itself of persons who become aware of events. That is, historical consciousness refers to *the set of assumptions,* or lenses, by which persons evaluate anything.

For example, until recently our consciousness about the colonization of the Americas was made up of a set of assumptions that
are solidly grounded in Western European classical culture. Among
these assumptions are: "White, baptized people are *ipso facto* superior in value to native peoples of whatever country. Colonization is
our right." In other words, we knew of events but had little historical consciousness, or better, little historical self-consciousness.
We presumed that our mental constructs for making sense of the
world were the best, if not the only ones. And so it seemed terrible
or inappropriate for native peoples to fight for their land when it
was obvious that taking it from them was our "manifest destiny."

At significant places in his work, John Henry Cardinal
Newman referred to the impact of "unspoken, unquestioned, operative [i.e., controlling] assumptions" upon conscious thought and
human behavior.[3] He indicated that these unspoken, unquestioned
attitudes or assumptions are powerful precisely because they are
preconscious, that is, below the level of our thinking about them.
Indeed, each of us was born into a set of assumptions about the
world and relationships in the world, that is, about "the way things
ought to be."[4] More recently, we have heard expressions like the
"classical worldview," and the "modern worldview," and that
increasing numbers of people are now living with a "post-modern
view of the world."

I offer some illustrations for the purpose of appreciation. At a
family gathering, a cousin asked about my activities. I told her that
I taught seminarians how to preside at Mass, that I regularly
preach and that I preside at Vespers. To which my cousin asked:
"Have you forgotten your place?"

Clearly, her dismay at my behavior was rooted in a complex
of assumptions about women and in her operative (controlling)
understanding of the origin of the church. She was quick to say
that the church came into being when Jesus ordained men at the
Last Supper and gave them the role of all leadership in the church.
Further, her statement is rooted in an unquestioned assumption
that the New Testament is a direct, eyewitness account. "And,"
she quipped, "if women would be more like Mary, we would not
have so much disorder in society!"

One could argue for some time and still not move the issue until my cousin examines her worldview and the assumptions about women and the formation of scripture that her conceptual paradigm presents. Upon examination, it would be clear that they are grounded in what we have come to call the classical worldview.

The Influence of Cosmology on Thought and Behavior

Our purpose is to reflect on various worldviews and then to bring these insights to bear on the current state of liturgical practice in the church.[5]

The Classical Worldview Paradigm

The classical worldview is associated with the influence of the philosophies of Plato and Aristotle in Mediterranean lands and on the European continent. In the fourth century before the common era, Alexander the Great, conqueror of the known world at that time, encouraged the spread of the philosophy of his tutor, Aristotle, as well as that of Plato. This classical paradigm conceived of the organization of reality according to ranks of being in the spiritual world as well as in the material world. The spiritual world was imaged in the shape of a pyramid, with God at the top, and in descending order, the angels and the souls of the dead. Further, it was thought that the material world had to mirror the spiritual world.

The biology of this worldview is significant. It was assumed that the entire person was contained in the male sperm and simply planted in the woman at the time of intercourse. The role of the woman in procreation was considered merely passive. Correlatively, the social role of women was passive. This social construct is known as "patriarchy" or "father rule."

The church has its historical roots in Judaism, which itself had a similar view of being and social reality. Hence, the church was born into a social atmosphere that did not regard women either as full persons according to the covenant or as full persons according to the philosophies of Aristotle or Plato.

We know from the historical-critical study of scripture that Jesus criticized this way of valuing persons and that with his resurrection, the very earliest insights about being Christian implied that the Jewish and classical views of persons were not consistent with the revelation of God in Christ. We note Galatians 3:28, our earliest baptismal hymn, and the fact that no separate initiation rites for males and females existed. If, however, we examine the documents of the New Testament in order of their composition, we clearly see that, as it spread into Hellenistic culture, the church rather uncritically absorbed the classical worldview of persons and social organization into its own theological thought, social structures and practice. This is certainly true regarding theology of worship and church structures of authority, as well as thought about the value and social role of women.

For example, shortly after the fall of the Roman empire (476 CE), a man who took the pen name of "Dionysious" wrote two books. *The Heavenly Hierarchy* described the spiritual world.[6] Therein, the risen Christ is seated at the right hand of God, and in descending order, the ranks of the angels and the souls of the just. The second book, *The Ecclesiastical Hierarchy,* assumed that the material world must mirror the spiritual world. At the pinnacle of the pyramid is the pope, and in descending order, the ranks of the clergy and all the baptized. This paradigm also contained the biological view noted earlier. These two texts would influence all subsequent theology in the church into this century.

In the late tenth and early eleventh centuries, the philosophical literature of Aristotle was reintroduced onto the European continent by Jewish and Arab philosophers, and it reinforced the classical worldview with all of its patriarchal assumptions. In addition to assuming that the author "Dionysious" was the companion of Paul at Athens (Acts 17:33), and therefore, it was assumed, an eyewitness of the structure of the church which he described in *The Ecclesiastical Hierarchy,* Saint Thomas and Saint Bonaventure, among others, based their respective theologies on the assumptions of the classical worldview articulated by "Dionysius."

In the *prima primae* of the *Summa Theologica*, question 92, Thomas considers the production (creation) of Woman. There, based on the teaching of Aristotle, Thomas speculates that, because the female is a physically misbegotten male, it is fitting that the male was created first. The reason why females are such physically is this: During intercourse, the male seed, which tends toward the production of a perfect likeness in the masculine sex, is somehow made defective, perhaps because of a moist south wind. And so, even though females share human nature through their souls, the misbegotten condition of their bodies makes them naturally subject to males. This kind of economic or civil subjection existed even before the Fall, because good order demands that women be governed by those who are wiser than themselves.[7] The history of canon law witnesses to the incorporation of these assumptions into church life. The 1917 *Code of Canon Law* implied that women could not be ordained because they were not sufficiently intelligent.[8]

Modern Worldview: The Age of Enlightenment

With the discoveries of Galileo and Copernicus in the late sixteenth and early seventeenth centuries, the above paradigm of reality received serious critique.[9] By the mid 1700s, the scientific or modern worldview was well on its way to showing the inadequacies of the classical worldview in several arenas. For example: historical-critical study of scripture challenged long-held views; that disease is caused by germs challenged the previously held notion that disease was punishment from God, and so on. From 1750 on, we note some other consequences of this modern view: the Industrial Revolution, as well as the demise of or serious reduction of the power of monarchies in Europe.

The American colonies declared independence from England in 1776 and embarked on the American Experiment: government of, by and for "the people."[10] And democracy was condemned by the church as a threat to the stability of society. Still, by the late 1800s, even the notion of "the people" articulated in the Declaration of Independence and the Constitution of the United States was challenged and expanded by the women's suffrage movement.[11]

In this century, the contributions of modern medicine and psychology overturned the classical view of the creation of both women and men by acknowledging the active role of the female egg along with the sperm in the procreation of human life. All of these scientifically proven data have led to the transformation of the teaching of the church on the meaning of marriage between man and woman. Today, we no longer speak of the primary ends of marriage as the procreation of children and the cure for concupiscence, but as a covenant between equals that is open to new life through mutual love and encouragement. Further, this century has witnessed the elections of Golda Meier as head of the State of Israel, of Margaret Thatcher of Britain, of Benezir Bhutto of Pakistan and of other women in every form of civil office. *It is only to be expected that the issue of women in various public offices in the church should be raised.*

The Post-Modern Exploration

Early in this century, scientists further challenged the findings of Copernicus and Galileo.[12] Today, we know that the sun is certainly the center of our galaxy, but we also know of many other galaxies, of black holes, of the expanding and contracting of galaxies and that, at the subatomic level, the very particles of our beings are related to every other particle of being in the universe.[13] We have witnessed the growth of global awareness that what happens to forests in Brazil affects our lives on the North American continent and beyond. Such are some of the findings of the new science, or what we call the "post-modern worldview." Pertinent to our consideration of the eucharist, we note that this view of reality can strike at all forms of authority, social norms or boundaries of any sort.

Consequences for the Liturgical Renewal

As ministers in the church, we are faced with this challenging fact: Many persons are still operating according to a classical worldview, resisting the most basic *positive* insights of the modern world, while still others are well on their way to appreciating the incompleteness of the modern view of things. These latter speak of living in a post-modern world. Appreciation of the current state of liturgical reform and spiritual renewal is directly related to appreciation of the fact that members of the church are operating out of one or a combination of worldviews or cosmologies, which in turn shape their views about the nature of the church, its public worship, authority and leadership, and certainly the significance of the feminist critique of theology and ecclesial practice.

Even if we do not consciously reflect on them, these data have an impact on our understanding of our lives, on our relationship to all of creation, and on how we conceive of God and the revelation of God in Jesus the Christ. They have an impact on how we value ourselves as human beings in general and as women and men in particular. They have an impact on what we are willing to tolerate or not in our relationships with each other in the Body of Christ in history, the church, as well as in our American society. The data of both the scientific worldview and the post-modern worldview (which do not completely negate all the values of the classical worldview) have stimulated questions today that were literally impossible to imagine in a church so profoundly penetrated by the values of the classical view of reality. So, to these questions we now turn.

Several phases mark the study of liturgy, from the study of the rubrics and the collection and editing of texts through form and redaction criticism, to the retrieval of the notion of public worship, that is, liturgical worship as "first theology" *(theologia prima)*. This latter approach recognizes that theory and practice cannot be validly separated; what persons do is an expression of what they believe. Hence, Augustine could argue that we need the grace of God for salvation because the church prays for that grace in its liturgy.

From the perspective of what persons have done at liturgical prayer over the centuries, this germinal insight has never been lost. However, prior to the period shortly before Vatican II, and with rare exception, theological treatises on the sacraments concentrated on the truth most clearly implied by the classical worldview:

In virtue of the life, death and resurrection of Jesus the Christ, the sacraments are a kind of instrumental cause by which God effects the grace that brings about our salvation. In this theological construct, the priest is yet another kind of instrumental cause who acts in the person of the heavenly Christ in the manner of an actor playing a role here on earth. In other words, the theology of the sacraments, as well as the associated catechesis, with which the church has been familiar until well into this century, has been a theological account shaped (controlled) by the cosmology and biology of the classical worldview.

As is clear, this theology was at pains to articulate that God in Christ is the ultimate efficient cause of the effects of the sacraments. In order to preserve this truth, theologians drew up an extended list of instrumental causes at the service of the efficient cause, God. In this synthesis, little explanatory attention is given to either the faith response of the assembly in the divine-human engagement or to the meaning of the human, social gathering as such. So long as scholasticism and neoscholasticism (rooted in the classical worldview) prevailed, the ordained priest could be understood to "say Mass for the people," and the other members of the assembly would not be deemed necessary for that performance. The sole reference to the members of the assembly was that they place no obstacle (that is, serious sin) to the conferral of grace for the worthy reception of the sacrament.

So powerful was this articulation, and its correlative implication of the non-necessity of the assembly for the liturgical act, that theology further asked and specified that the bare minimum for the confecting of the sacrament is the recitation of the "form," words attributed to Jesus, in relation to the matter, bread and wine. Although the Canon of the Mass (eucharistic prayer) was recited, it was not considered an essential element (instrumental cause) in the process, nor was the proclamation of the scriptures or preaching. Even though Saint Thomas did not directly encourage the arbitrary (one could say promiscuous) confecting of the sacrament, he logically concluded that the words of a priest, if he directed the words of institution toward bread in a bakery, would thereby confect the sacrament.

Theresa F. Koernke, IHM

These narrow theological emphases on the role of the ministerial priest and the words of institution created fallow ground for
disregarding the deep structure of the entire eucharistic liturgy. If, in
this conceptual atmosphere, all that really matters is what the priest
says in relation to the bread and cup, then it is understandable, if
regrettable, that clergy felt free to add to or diverge from the basic
pattern of the Mass. Indeed, such performative aberrations jeop-
ardized the objective meaning of the Mass: God in Christ acting
to save us. In that milieu, Luther and Calvin were correct in observ-
ing that the manner in which the Mass was performed implied that
priests controlled the grace of God. Although this was never the
formal teaching of the church, it seemed that the performance of
these actions controlled God by their mere performance — a
skewed understanding of *ex opere operato.* Hence, the protesting
reformers accused the church of encouraging "works righteousness," the idea that one is justified or saved precisely by performing
these works, the sacraments.

In reaction to these liturgical abuses, the reformers took the
worst of Catholic practices to their ultimate conclusion: The
eucharistic prayer was removed, leaving only the words of institution (in an appearance of fidelity to the scriptures), and the sovereignty of God was hailed in the proclamation of the word and in
preaching.

The bishops at the Council of Trent (1545 – 1563), during the
Counter-Reformation, responded with the 1570 revision of the
Roman Missal, which included directions printed in red ("rubrics").
These rubrics were intended to preserve the Rite of the Mass from
aberration, as well as to preserve the assembly from the personal
idiosyncrasies of the clergy (what I have called performative hetero-
doxy, or *performative heresy*).[14] Given these rampant abuses, as
well as widespread popular superstitions, Trent mandated the
observance of these directives printed in red as necessary for the
validity of the sacrament.

Although certainly not expanded on in the documents of Trent,
there was a seminal insight here regarding *signification,* or meaning, that would not come to full flowering until this century. Even
though the church had taught *sacramenta significando causant,*

"the sacraments cause grace precisely *by signifying,*" or meaning grace, theological treatises had only considered the fact and manner in which God effects or causes grace through them. In short, scholastic systematic theology made no worthy account either of the fact that the entire complex of signs (space, language, gesture, etc.) bears meaning precisely to persons or of the fact that persons engage in the subjective appropriation of meaning. This critique of scholastic systematic theology is first of all an observation of appreciation; the cosmology of the classical worldview, with its extreme emphasis on the sovereignty of God and a narrow anthropology, literally controlled both the questions asked and the possible responses.

From the late seventeenth and early eighteenth centuries on, there is no doubt that the scientific methods of the modern worldview have benefited our study of the liturgy. Through comparative studies of liturgical texts, scholars like Anton Baumstock, Robert Taft, Gabrielle Winkler and Balthasar Fischer have demonstrated the fruitful result of literary textual, form and redaction criticisms. Their historical-textual studies have, for example, spearheaded the return of the Easter Vigil to its rightful place on Holy Saturday (rather than in the morning!), as well as the retrieval of the full catechumenate and the very reform of the liturgy of the sacraments.

In addition to the historical-textual studies, the rise of the scientific study of the liturgy has also witnessed the use of data from psychology, sociology, language theory, semiotics and various aspects of anthropology, especially ritual studies.[15] From these data I would set out the following reflections on "Eucharist: From Rubricism to Freedom."

Eucharist: From Rubricism to Freedom

Paragraph 7 of the *Constitution on the Sacred Liturgy* witnesses to a retrieval of the tradition by reintroducing attention to the power of the rites to mean or signify:

Theresa F. Koernke, IHM

> The liturgy . . . is rightly seen as an exercise of the priestly office of Jesus Christ. It involves the presentation of humanity's sanctification *under the guise of signs perceptible by the senses and its accomplishment in ways appropriate to each of these signs.* (emphasis mine)

In other words, by the embrace of the Spirit in initiation, all the baptized are joined together and to Christ *in his total self-offering (sacrifice) to God,* that is, in his obedience unto death. The church, therefore, has its origin as a whole from the bestowal of the Spirit by Jesus the Christ. As Paul so often reminded the churches: You have been plunged into the death of the Lord by the power of the Spirit to the worship of God.

As social beings, the disciples of Jesus have gathered to call to mind — to make *anamnesis* of — their origin in the self-offering of Jesus through the celebration of the Lord's Supper. The liturgy — the action of the baptized — is rightly seen as an exercise — an actualization — of the priestly office/duty of Jesus Christ, in and through the assembly, using signs appropriate to the meaning of that eucharistic action.

What follows is a reflection on the objective meaning of the "depth structure"[16] of the liturgy of the Mass. Its purpose is to create a context in which we can evaluate our praxis of the liturgy, to see if we have really moved from undue attention to rubrics to genuine freedom within the context of the meaning of the eucharist.

Today we are in the position to avail ourselves of myriad data about the eucharist. What knowledge will enable a disposition of freedom from rubricism and a freedom for eucharist for the sake of the peace and salvation of all the world?

Most of us would agree that a kind of rubricism is associated with the traditionalist movement and its nostalgic attachment to the Tridentine Mass. However, I would suggest that, for all of the data available to those of us who consider ourselves open to the liturgical movement, an assumption of the classical-Tridentine view of the eucharist continues to hold us, far more than may be obvious. Indeed, a review of the depth structure (underlying yet accessible dynamic) or primordial divine-human pattern of the eucharist, from out of a modern and postmodern worldview, may better enable us to name the behaviors that continue to reflect that former classical view (on one hand) and those that are grounded in the freedom of the deep structure of the eucharist.

At the heart of the Judaic biblical tradition is the conviction that God acts first in creation and redemption. By the breath of God, the Word of God has brought forth creation. By the breath of God, that Word continues to speak through the law, the covenant and the prophets. By the breath of God, the people respond to God, who continues to speak through the scriptures and whose creation and covenant is called to mind on festive occasions through the celebration of a ritual meal. Hearing God speak and responding to God is the primordial pattern of human worship.

Our Christian ancestors reflected this primordial pattern by joining the hearing of the scriptures with the ritual meal in which the human response of praise and thanksgiving is given to God, now in Christ, by the power of the Spirit. The purpose of those gatherings was not to see how differently the celebration could be done but to dispose oneself to hear the Word, the Christ, and to respond to God in Christ. The host of those gatherings was not understood to be the bishop or presbyter but Christ present by the power of the Spirit in the members of the assembly. *This context determines what is done (or not) and what is understood.* What if there were never any directives written in red?

Liturgy of the Word

We know that the early Christians continued to hear the scriptures of the Old Covenant but heard them now through the lens of their experience of the risen Lord. And as the letters of Paul and the gospels were composed and collected, these as well were heard in the assembly. The conviction then, and now, as noted in the *General Instruction of the Roman Missal,* is this: God continues to speak through the proclamation of the scriptures, and Christ, present among us, speaks to his body, the church.

We know that as the classical worldview took hold and greater emphasis was given to how God acts in the Mass that the liturgy of the word received little theological attention, and preaching doctrines took the place of the mystagogical homily. However, now that the liturgy of the word has been richly retrieved, what if there were no directives written in red? With which worldview would we, have we, do we, celebrate it?

The Liturgy of the Eucharist

In his study *The Eucharistic Prayers of the Roman Rite,* Enrico Mazza[17] sets out the process of development from a meal which Jesus ate with his disciples toward the end of his life. He notes that on certain festive occasions, like the feast of Purim and the Passover, meals of bodily satisfaction were punctuated by blessings over bread and cups of wine.

In this context, the leader took bread, blessed God for all the great acts of creation and redemption, especially for creating the people with whom God is always present, and passed the bread in silence. Any good Jew would have understood that to eat of this bread was to eat the history of the people, to take the people whom God had created into themselves, to reaffirm their belonging, not simply to God but to God with all the people. Then, at the conclusion of the meal, the leader took a final cup, praised and blessed God for the covenant and for the privilege of keeping the law, and passed the cup in silence. In this context, any good Jew would have understood that to drink of the cup was to drink in the covenant made by God with the people, to reaffirm the covenant that God made, to thank God for the privilege of keeping the Law of the covenant, to give oneself yet again to the norms that govern a moral life. And then (as the rabbis taught), having told God all that God needs to hear, the final prayer asks that God hear and respond to the needs of the people. Quite simply, this pattern of prayer is the origin of the eucharistic prayer.

As Mazza suggests, toward the end of his life Jesus gathered with his disciples to eat a ritual meal. During grace before the meal, Jesus took bread, prayed the lengthy blessing of God over it, and passed it around. Here, Jesus broke the silence and said: "Take, eat. This [is] my body for you." At the end of the meal, he then took the cup, prayed the blessing of God for having given the covenant, and passed the cup. Again, Jesus broke the usual silence and said: "This cup [is the] new covenant in my blood." Then followed the prayer that God hear the prayers of the people.

As Jews, the disciples of Jesus most certainly were shocked, not simply because Jesus broke the silence but by what he said. If for centuries they and their ancestors had consumed that bread with the conviction that they were eating the history of their people created by God, the words of Jesus transformed the meaning of that eating. Here, Jesus had associated himself with God, who creates a new people. Eating this bread now is to eat the history of the people created by the act of God in the life of Jesus. And, if for centuries they and their ancestors had drunk from that cup with the conviction that they were reaffirming the covenant made by God at Sinai, and delighting in being able to keep the Law, the words of Jesus transformed the meaning of that drinking. Here, Jesus had associated himself with God, who redeems by bringing the people out of slavery and by making a covenant that demands moral behavior.

It seems clear that the disciples of Jesus could not, all at once, grasp the terror and delight associated with his breaking of silence. And perhaps this shock, along with having a price, led Judas to sell out. In any case, historical-critical study of Jewish prayers at the time of Jesus, in comparison with the accounts of institution, enable us to reach into our collective history by the power of the Spirit and to retrieve the magnificence and power of those accounts of institution.

So long as the mission of the church remained among "the descendants of Abraham and Moses" there would have been no need to tell Jewish Christians to repeat this meal. It would have been understood. There would have been no need for "printed directives." However, when the mission spread into Hellenistic culture — which had no such understanding of blessing God over bread and cup — a directive to repeat this form of blessing and eating was needed. And so we note that, in the First Letter of Paul to the Corinthians, we find perhaps the earliest liturgical directive, grounded on the experience of the risen Jesus and the knowledge of his desire: "Do this in my memory." Paul needed to tell these non-Jewish Christians that "whenever we eat this bread and drink this cup, we proclaim the death of the Lord until he comes."

Today, the directives printed in red are not there to stifle but to preserve the people of God from the whims of either the presider or the parish liturgy committee. Sometimes we need them to ensure that what we do, we do according to the meaning of the deep structure. Indeed, Paul needed to recatechize the Corinthians about the meaning of what they were doing. And the need for re-catechizing continues. Today, the eucharistic prayer addresses God, to whom all creation rightly gives praise. It recounts the great works of creation and redemption, the greatest of which is the life, death and resurrection of Jesus the Christ, who gave us a new way of worshiping God. For this reason, we say, we bring God gifts and ask that they be made holy, so that they may become for us a true participation in the whole Christ, head and members, and true participation in the blood of Christ, that is, in the self-offering of Christ on the cross.

Obviously, "body and blood" are metaphors referring to the person of Christ, who has given himself unto death. And if the Christ can never be separated from the members of the corporate body, when the church prays "Let your Spirit come upon these gifts that they may become for us a true encounter with the Christ," and when we receive communion, we can never say that the encounter is solely an individual encounter with the individual Jesus the Christ.

We note all this in order to say that what we have thought about the liturgy of the word and about the eucharistic prayer has determined the behavior of the presider and the other members of the assembly. We could be absent from the liturgy of the word and still fulfill our Sunday obligation, and even though we kept the entire canon, it was prayed quietly and great attention was given to the words of institution, the presider taking the role of Jesus at the Last Supper. Now then, even though the eucharistic prayer is addressed to God, our classical cosmology led us to basically disregard that fact in our theological account. We really did not see the canon as a prayer of praise and thanksgiving. Indeed, at the words of institution, the rubrics said that the priest consciously associated himself with Christ at the Last Supper! The institution narrative was turned into a play of Christ at the Last Supper.

The worldview that sustained that narrow interpretation of the accounts of institution is still present among us in the manner in which presiders abruptly shift from proclaiming a prayer of praise and thanksgiving to assuming the role of Jesus at the Last Supper, addressing the assembly rather than simply recalling to God the deeds of Jesus. We note breaking the bread at the words of institution and the turning about for all to see the elements rather than realizing that uplifted arms in prayer is the posture of the eucharistic prayer.

We are, quite simply, still in the process of moving out of the classical worldview, attempting to take seriously the data of biblical scholarship of the modern world, so that we might genuinely retrieve the deep structure of the full celebration of the eucharist. In short, the best way to move beyond rubricism to genuine freedom in the celebration of the eucharist is to recapture the deep structure that leads to freedom for the hearing of the word and to the praise of God through, with and in the Word made flesh by the power of the Spirit.

1. See Gilbert Ostdiek, "Ritual and Transformation: Reflections on Liturgy and the Social Sciences," *Liturgical Ministry* 2 (Spring 1993): 38–48.

2. See Eric Erikson, "The Development of Ritualization," in *The Religious Situation* (Boston: Beacon Press, 1968): 711–733.

3. John Henry Newman, *Grammar of Assent* (London: Longmans, Green and Co., 1903): 60, and *Lectures on the Present Position of Catholics in England* (Dublin: 1857): 26.

4. Recall such social mores as: women always need head-covering in church; only males may serve as acolytes or preach, etc.

5. See Robin W. Lovin and Frank E. Reynolds, "In the Beginning," in *Cosmogony and Ethical Order: New Studies in Comparative Ethics,* ed. Lovin and Reynolds (Chicago: University of Chicago Press, 1985): 1–35; N. Max Wildiers, *The Theologian and His Universe: Theology and Cosmology from the Middle Ages to the Present* (New York: Seabury, 1982).

6. Dionysious the Pseudo-Areopagite, *The Ecclesiastical Hierarchy,* trans. and notes Thomas L. Campbell, CSC (Washington, D.C.: University Press of America, 1981).

7. Thomas Aquinas, *Summa Theologica* I, I, question 92, articles 1 – 4.

8. See canons 968 – 982 of the 1917 *Code of Canon Law.*

9. Copernicus dedicated *The Revolution of the Terrestrial Orbs* (1543) to the Pope: "It is not the sun which revolves around the earth but the earth which turns on itself and around the sun." A half-century later, problems arose when Copernican "heliocentrism" is taken up by Giordano Bruno and Galileo. It seemed to contradict Genesis, Ecclesiastes 1:4 – 5, and Joshua 10:12 – 13.

10. Like most philosophers of his time, Thomas Jefferson was a Deist who acknowledged a natural religion which did not oppose reason, but rejected revelation. In this view, the "divine right" of monarch's is inconsistent with reason; hence the "American experiment" was conceived as government of, by and for the people.

11. See Ellen C. DuBois, *Feminism and Suffrage: The Emergence of an Independent Women's Movement in America,* 1848 – 1869 (1978); Eleanor Flexner, *Century of Struggle: The Women's Rights Movement in the United States,* rev. ed. (1975).

12. For these developments, see Robert M. Gascoigne, "The New Cosmology: Science Ponders Divine Creation" The *Australasian Catholic Record* 71 (July 1994): 330 – 340.

13. Margaret J. Wheatley, *Leadership and the New Science: Learning About Organization from an Orderly Universe* (San Francisco: Berrett-Koehler Publishers, 1992).

14. Theresa F. Koernke, "Toward an Ethics of Liturgical Behavior," *Worship* 66 (1992): 25 – 38, esp. 31.

15. Ostdiek, "Ritual and Transformation."

16. I am grateful to Joyce Ann Zimmerman, *Liturgy as Living Faith: A Liturgical Spirituality* (Scranton: University of Scranton Press, 1993), who uses the terms depth structure and depth meaning from the work of textual analysis set out by Paul Ricoeur.

17. Enrico Mazza, *The Eucharistic Prayers of the Roman Rite,* trans. Matthew J. O'Connell (New York: Pueblo Publishing Co., 1986).

Catherine Vincie, RSHM

Liturgy and Justice: Keeping the Connections Alive

Making the connections between liturgy and justice continues to be one of the critical issues in contemporary religious thought and practice. A look at how the North American church broached this subject earlier this century and during the Second Vatican Council is a good starting point. Hindsight provides a certain clarity about where we've been, where we stand now and possibilities for the future. This paper will consider the connections between liturgy and justice in the pioneering influence of Virgil Michel, in the teachings of Vatican II, in the reception of the conciliar teachings, as well as consider some of the tensions, concerns and issues that remain in discerning the connections between liturgy and justice.

The Legacy of Virgil Michel

Father Virgil Michel, Benedictine priest, educator, author, editor and architect of the North American liturgical reform movement, was without doubt an important wisdom figure for the church during the second and third decades of this century.[1] He died in 1938, after only 48 short but enormously busy years; Michel helped to make the developments in the European liturgical movement available in this country. But he did much more than that. Father Michel tried to hold together a revitalized liturgical life and a passion for social regeneration, something the European movement had not addressed.

Michel was keenly aware that Christianity existed in the world and had a role to play in its evolving history. Addressing the particular challenges of the period between the two world wars, Michel was convinced that the dark side of individualism, collectivism and totalitarianism needed to be confronted and that the Christian gospel could provide an alternative vision. In particular, Michel was sure that the liturgy could serve as the foundation for a new social order because it was "the primary source of the true Christian Spirit."[2] The liturgy's communal character provided an antidote to the pathologies of both Western and Eastern North Atlantic political, social and economic systems. Father Michel was not a systematic theologian, nor did he have available to him the fruit of symbolic and ritual studies that would come in later decades. Nonetheless, he had the instincts to begin with the symbolic language of the liturgy and with foundational images of the church to make the connections between liturgy and justice.

On the one hand, Michel argued that the communal experience of corporate liturgy, such as it was before the council, had the potential to shape a communal consciousness within the participants. On the other hand, he also employed a new image for the church emerging out of the European context at the time: The church as the Mystical Body of Christ. This provided Michel with an image for the solidarity of the Christian with Christ, with the whole church and with all others.

Michel's concern for a reinvigorated liturgical life did not necessarily push him toward extensive liturgical reforms, although he certainly advocated gradual liturgical evolution. Rather, he was convinced that by entering more deeply into the spirit of the liturgy and with better understanding, the Christian community could transform the culture of individualism and collectivism. While participation in the liturgy and participation in the construction of a new social order were two sides of the same coin of Christian discipleship, it is legitimate to argue that Michel made the connection between liturgy and justice by beginning with the liturgy as source for a new social order. In retrospect, one might even suggest that there was a certain naiveté in his expectation that the liturgy, in the form which he knew it then, was adequate to the task. Nonetheless, Michel's passion for connecting worship with social regeneration is a solid foundation on which we can still rely.

The Second Vatican Council

The *Constitution on the Sacred Liturgy* is notable for its attempt to connect the liturgy with ecclesiology and with christology. In it we read that the liturgy manifests and effects the church; that the liturgy is an exercise of the priestly office of Jesus Christ; that liturgical celebrations are an action of Christ and of the church. The constitution specifically stresses the communal and public character of the liturgy while also calling for greater participation. The symbolic nature of liturgy is highlighted, as is the formative nature of our celebrations. The fact that the constitution has radically reshaped our liturgical life is undeniable, even if the evaluation of those changes is still debated.

Unfortunately, Virgil Michel's vision of the connection between liturgy and justice did not find its way into this reform document for the universal church. Perhaps Michel's untimely death and the dominance during the conciliar process of European liturgical reformers, who were not as passionate about these connections, were responsible for this unfortunate gap. Whatever the reasons, the legacy of the conciliar liturgical reform has been a concerted effort to reform the liturgies for the expressed purpose of revitalizing Christian life, without any expressed connection between worship and justice.

The "blame" lies not only with the formulators of the liturgy constitution. The *Dogmatic Constitution on the Church (Lumen gentium)* and the *Pastoral Constitution on the Church in the Modern World (Gaudium et spes)* were equally responsible for the bifurcation between worship and Christian action for justice. These two conciliar documents on the church made great strides in inserting the Catholic church into the mainstream of Western thought and culture after several centuries of isolation and suspicion. While

Karl Rahner pointed to Vatican II as the turning point in the church becoming a world church, at the time of the council the integration of the developments of even Western thought had yet to be achieved.

Looking back over the last thirty years, we can see that while modernity was coming to an end at the time of the council and beyond, the church was only beginning to engage in dialogue with it. The overly optimistic approach to the world in the council's documents on the church stems from a late, but necessary, embracing of modernity even while its limitations were clearly rising on the horizon. The domination of scientific reasoning, technology at the price of ecological destruction, individual exploitation for either capitalistic or socialistic ends, the marginalization of religion and the arts all point to a need to move beyond the limits of modernity. While the gift of the council was to thrust the church back into dialogue with the world, it would nevertheless take some time to learn the languages of modernity and then to move beyond it.

While inserting the church into the modern world and embracing the hopes and concerns of all humanity, the framers of these two conciliar documents on the church failed to include worship in their deliberations. *Gaudium et spes* particularly argues for the work of human betterment and social involvement as constitutive elements of the church's mission. Yet the connection between worship (also a constitutive element of the church) and social involvement was left completely unexplored. While one may argue that conciliar teaching must be taken as a whole, the failure of the council to link these two concerns within each document was an unfortunate and costly oversight.

Conciliar Reception

The reception and implementation of the conciliar agenda was and continues to be a monumental task. With so much work to be done in the immediate postconciliar period, distinct groups within the church chose their focus. By choice or temperament or simply by the limits of time and energy, social activists and liturgical reformers engaged in the enormous task of revision and reconstruction in their respective areas, quite independently of one another, and, at times, with a fair amount of antipathy towards one another.

Literature on the reception of ecclesial councils suggests that local churches selectively and creatively choose — from the myriad teaching that comes forth from a council — those particular issues that are vital to its life.[3] Rather than viewing such choices as a failure in breadth, the selection process may be viewed as a grace of insight, a Spirit-grounded response by groups trying to live in the particularity of a given situation. Thus, it is easier to appreciate the phenomenon that in the first 25 years after the council, subgroups within the U.S. and Canadian local churches selectively, creatively and independently received the council's mandate for liturgical reform, on the one hand, and ecclesial renewal regarding social justice, on the other. Each group engaged in the task of reform and renewal with enthusiasm and energy precisely because those individuals and groups were convinced that their select element of conciliar teaching was absolutely vital to the church's life. Perhaps because of the magnitude of each task, neither sub-group seemed to engage in both tasks simultaneously, and nothing in the conciliar texts demanded that they do so.

In a generous interpretation of such developments, one could say that the church, as an organic body and one with a multiplicity of charisms, can and ought to be involved in a rich diversity of concerns and ministries, since together they constitute the fullness of Christian discipleship. Yet to select single elements from among the church's constitutive dimensions bears intrinsic limits. While appreciating the gift of selection and focus, we must also admit that during the first decades after the council, holding together the various strands of Christian life, such as liturgy and justice, was either not possible or not valued, or both.

In what I view as a positive development, there has been increasing discomfort with an exclusively either/or approach to justice and the liturgy. Perhaps the growth and developments in both areas have now been sufficient to allow the integration of subgroups themselves or an integration of these elements within

individuals. If this is not true across the board, at least we are seeing more demands for their integration now than we saw in the
preceding years. Integration is the emerging value.

Postconciliar Developments
Regarding Liturgy and Justice

While it is impossible to specify the turning point toward greater
integration of liturgy and justice, it is clear that the 1980s saw a
preponderance of literature attempting to broach the subject.[4]
Attention to this concern even expanded in the 1990s. Six trends
mark these postconciliar developments, particularly from a liturgical perspective. This section will focus on developments that are
primarily positive, at least in the sense that they are attempts to
establish or foster the connection between liturgy and justice.

In an attempt to uncover patterns in this vast literature, I have
chosen to take core samples from the field. That is, I have chosen
individual articles or parts thereof that either pull together new
insights or suggest new and fruitful explorations. By taking specific articles as examples of each trend, I have necessarily oversim-
plified their content and perhaps made some arbitrary assignments
to one category rather than to another. My concern is to be sug-
gestive rather than exhaustive, and I apologize to those authors
whose work is more comprehensive than my analysis here allows.

The Baptized as the Subject of the Church's Mission and of the Liturgy

The council shifted the responsibility for Christian life and ministry from the hierarchy to all the baptized and taught that the
whole gathered church is the subject of the liturgy. Therefore, questions of ecclesial action for justice and authentic worship have
become more pressing for the entire baptized community. This new
self-understanding of the church replaced an ecclesiology that put
the overall mission of the church and its worship primarily in the
hands of the hierarchy. The merely baptized assimilated themselves

to the work of the priestly hierarchy as best they could. It could be argued that some, such as Virgil Michel, espoused the more participatory ecclesiology of the council earlier on, at least in general terms. However, it became official church teaching in the conciliar documents, and the reception of this teaching by the baptized has made it a living reality in ways that simply were not true before. This shift to a conscious sense of responsibility by the baptized for the church's mission and its worship has affected how justice and liturgy are addressed.

The feminist biblical scholar Elisabeth Schüssler Fiorenza gives witness to the degree of conciliar reception of this ecclesiology in an important *Concilium* article on tablesharing and the eucharist.[5] In this article, she assumes that the whole people of God celebrates the liturgy, and as church, incarnates itself in the eucharist, even as she decries the degree to which we have taken the implications of this seriously. Specific to our concerns, she argues that overcoming societal discrimination and prejudice and establishing equality in ecclesial tablesharing is a precondition for authentic eucharistic practice. Only Christian subjects who are acting justly outside of liturgical celebration as the expression of their baptismal identity can gather at the eucharistic table without condemnation. Schüssler Fiorenza's implicit conclusion is that *justice and liturgical authenticity is an issue for all the baptized.* Just action, she concludes, is a precondition for authentic worship. This is contingent upon establishing equality in ecclesial table sharing.

Fullness of Symbols and the Dark Side of Liturgy

The shift to fuller symbolic expression in liturgical celebration has led to a much greater appreciation of the quality of liturgical celebration itself. If the preconciliar period emphasized the action of Christ in the liturgy, the postconciliar period has stressed that the liturgy is both the action of Christ and human action, the action of the church. An emphasis on the latter has allowed us to see with much greater clarity the historical, social and cultural conditioning of all liturgical celebration. Our worship bears the marks of human genius and creativity as well as the inadequacies, biases and limitations of our vision. Honest reflection upon the liturgy has led us to admit that the liturgy can and does have a dark side. Liturgy can be the place where sinful structures and attitudes are writ in symbol form, invested with divine authority and surrounded with unspoken assumptions of God's presence. We have been forced to ask with Marjorie Procter-Smith whether "liturgy 'translate[s] violence' into beautiful forms."[6]

This deeper appropriation of the symbolic nature of liturgy has thus led us to conclude that *worship itself must be an act of justice*. Patterns of participation, ordering, position in space, authority to speak, to touch, move and use liturgical symbols all speak of social relations. The language of worship is also shaped by culture and by those who have power to decide. Thus our worship can be a manifestation of right relations among the baptized community; it can also be the means of communicating and reinforcing patterns of domination and discrimination, or a means of misusing power and authority. Cloaking these abuses in the ritual garments of solemnity, beauty of style, sound and space only serves to hide their dark side, making it more difficult to see and transform them. The critical questions of liturgical theology bring the discussion of justice into the framework of worship itself.

Symbols Unmasked — Layers of Injustice

Turning to the liturgy as a source of reflection on justice has led some authors to ask even more penetrating questions about the relationship between liturgy and justice. Enrique Dussel begins with the symbols of the liturgy, in his case the eucharistic symbol of bread, and asks us to think about the meaning of eucharist from the bread sign.[7] His approach does not allow us to naively assume that breaking bread in memory of Jesus Christ is communion in the body. For him, beginning with the bread sign means asking about the economic, social and political contexts that brought the bread from field to table. Is economic or cultural exploitation in any form responsible for the signs, symbols, music, art and environment of our worship?

He probes the authenticity of the celebration by looking intently at the symbols, so intently that we can see into the multiple layers of the symbols. *Here again, beauty may mask the violence of injustice in layers just beneath the liturgical celebration itself.*

Liturgy as Resource for Learning God's Ways of Justice

Attention to the celebration of the liturgy has led us into other fruitful areas of reflection. While I have suggested that liturgy has a dark side which we ignore at our peril, it also can be a place of revelation of the ways of justice. In other words, in exploring the connections between the liturgy and justice, some authors suggest that the liturgy leads us in the ways of justice.

We are invited by Mary Collins, for example, to turn to liturgical memorial and to the symbol of the eucharistic cup to learn God's ways of justice.[8] Convinced of its formative power, she begins with the liturgy and argues that it holds an important key to the integration of justice-ministry into an authentic Christian life. Liturgy serves as a reminder that God's justice and God's response to suffering in Jesus Christ are at the heart of Christian action for justice. The eucharistic liturgy, in particular, sets out for the community and rehearses the community over a lifetime in the memory of God's action in Jesus Christ.[9] The implication for those who keep memory of Jesus Christ in worship is that God's ways of justice are to become our ways of justice. The liturgy, through its symbolic forms, makes a distinctive contribution to Christian formation.

Collins reminds us, however, that distorted liturgical praxis can just as easily alienate the assembly from its core beliefs. Eucharistic practice that marginalizes the assembly from its ritual remembrance places an obstacle in the way of its ability to integrate both worship and action for justice as constitutive dimensions of the gospel. A revised eucharistic praxis that places the key actions of eucharistic taking, blessing, breaking and sharing in the hands of the assembly goes hand in hand with the authenticity of Christian life. In particular, actual sharing in the cup of suffering and blessing by the assembly and ongoing reflection on the experience has the potential for forming a community of just disciples.

The need to integrate liturgical renewal and action for justice goes beyond the practical need to address one aspect of the conciliar teaching and, when we can manage it, another. There is an internal necessity in Christian faith to hold together a discipleship of right worship — think "liturgical anamnesis" here — with a discipleship of justice. Yet even beyond this, Collins points to *the primacy of liturgy as a source for learning the ways of justice if all the baptized celebrate well.*

Revised Liturgical Praxis in a Postmodern Age

A critical approach to the exploration of liturgy's role in forming just disciples has led to other questions about the adequacy of the liturgical reforms. The revised liturgical books brought forth many prayers from the Christian tradition of both East and West, as well as new ones. However, these texts, both old and new, were written at a time when concern for justice was not acute. For those who feel the urgency of contemporary justice concerns, much of our revised liturgical life rings hollow. I have argued that the revised proper prefaces (to cite one case) need even further and continuous revision as the believing community expands its understanding of how Jesus reveals God's ways of justice.[10] But this is only the tip of the iceberg.

The issue is not even that now there is an explicit concern for justice and previously there was not. More importantly, our whole worldview has changed. Our understanding of history, our sense of responsibility for social, economic and political systems, our relationship with the earth and cosmos, and our understanding of the church's role in all these concerns have significantly changed since the council. Our coming to terms with the failures of modernity, and our beginning efforts to look at the public character of the church and its worship as a civic responsibility in this postmodern age are emerging as important avenues of concern.[11] *These new insights and changes in worldview, in the public character of the church and in worship as a public service, are what must be integrated into our liturgical forms if we hope to keep the connection between justice and worship alive.*

Making and Keeping Connections

While many have turned their attention to the formative and transformative power of liturgy, symbol and ritual, we know that liturgy simply cannot and ought not bear the total responsibility for shaping just disciples. To suggest that liturgy has such power ignores the complexity of human experience, individual and social, as well as the limitations of any single aspect of gospel living. At the same time, we cannot continue in the limited perspective of the council, where liturgy and action for justice remain discrete and unconnected units. While I have argued elsewhere for the need for creative catechists to make connections between worship and just discipleship,[12] *it is incumbent that all ecclesial ministries seek ways of holding the church's public worship in dialogue with their particular concerns.* While the interdisciplinary character of liturgical studies fosters such links, it is equally important that those working in other ecclesial disciplines and ministries turn their creative efforts toward making such links as well.

Present Tensions

I have outlined what I see as the significant trends that have emerged in the last two decades. I have deliberately focused on the positive developments that are fostering the integration of liturgical reform and ecclesial reform regarding action for justice. The picture, however, is not uniformly bright. There are tensions and problems that prevent the connections between liturgy and justice from being made, and from developing and even thriving. In the following section I will outline several of my concerns.

My first concern is that official liturgies would go on as usual without any efforts to integrate evolving justice issues. I am not convinced that the integration of evolving justice issues with the church's official liturgies has been taken seriously by those responsible for the ongoing revisions of the liturgical books. I agree with Kenneth Himes in his judgment that "[u]nless and until the concern for justice is integrated with the central spiritual exercise of the gathered community, there will remain a sense that the social ministry of the church is an adjunct, not a constitutive dimension of gospel life."[13]

Catherine Vincie, RSHM

My second concern is that superficial adjustments are made to the liturgy by the addition of a justice "theme" here and there. There is a need to incorporate into our liturgical celebrations the significant changes in a postmodern worldview that are affecting other aspects of ecclesial life. This means rethinking forms of participation in the church, in the liturgy and of the church in the world. It also means rethinking and reimaging the world, divine mystery, grace and human action, and bringing all of these to expression in our worship.

My third concern it that a parallel liturgical life is taking shape independent of and not influencing official liturgy. Unless the creative ritualizing that, in fact, is going on in small communities is taken seriously and valued, the wider church will miss an important opportunity to learn from some of its more creative and passionate members. We will simply widen the gap that exists between official liturgy and popular devotions. The cry for justice is being sounded, and it is finding a voice in ritual form but often privately or in isolated groups. On the one hand, such privacy is essential to allow creativity to emerge at its own pace. On the other hand, suspicion and inflammatory rhetoric from official ecclesial circles about these groups make the integration of their work exceedingly difficult. Those who shape future liturgical changes must learn to incorporate these new forms, images and symbols lest those concerned for justice lose confidence that the official public worship of the church is capable of proclaiming the justice of the gospel life.

My fourth concern is that our community, which is increasingly interested in developing a spiritual life that explicitly incorporates social action, is doing so without linkage to the liturgical, especially eucharistic, life of the church. Unless we can come to a new appreciation of corporate public worship as a constitutive dimension of gospel living, we risk creating another generation of those who focus on justice and those who focus on liturgy walking independently of one another. Or, perhaps, we risk creating a church convinced of a discipleship of justice but not convinced of the need to be a community of just disciples who gather for corporate public praise.

My fifth concern is that our liturgies continue to be a source of oppression at some times and in some areas. Our willingness to recognize the "dark side" of liturgy at the theoretical level has not led to the concrete elimination of aspects of injustice within liturgical celebrations. Because of the development of Roman Catholic liturgical forms primarily within North Atlantic Western culture, ways of naming reality, patterns of participation and leadership, as well as the shape of symbols, rituals and art forms have left little room for cultural, racial, ethnic and gender diversity to find its voice. The invisibility of the non-normative "other" has increasingly become understood as a matter of grave injustice.

The Future Agenda

My expectations for the future flow out of the trends and the concerns noted above. In the most general terms, the shift to a more phenomenological approach to worship has contributed greatly to our understanding of the liturgy as a place where justice may or may not be exercised. It has also increased our awareness of how the liturgy can form just disciples. Whatever the achievements of this new approach, we clearly have much more to learn, and developments in this area will bear on the topic of justice.

If Virgil Michel's approach was to see in the liturgy a new social vision, the postconciliar period is marked by an effort to move in both directions. While some efforts have already been made to attend to their mutual influence, I believe that the future agenda lies especially in attending to how a deepening understanding of justice challenges our public worship. This implies learning from many constituencies within the church, from other religious traditions and from those who claim no religious affiliation.

The efforts for greater inculturation of Christianity and its public worship will result in greater particularity in the ways local churches integrate their justice concerns and their worship. There will be no single answer always applicable to every local church. As I argued above, the desire to forge connections between various aspects of our life of discipleship is essentially sound and is a

Catherine Vincie, RSHM

continuing task for all local churches. However, the diversity of a "world church" and our willingness to learn from one another has the potential for enlarging our vision. Hearing one another across differences, either locally or worldwide, and listening to the marginalized, the alienated, the poor and the suffering is and will be important if we are to forge new links between liturgy and justice, links not previously imagined or even perceived as necessary. Since no single culture can express the totality of what it means to be human, the challenge of diversity suggests many new areas of development between liturgy and justice.

Continued interest in the formative character of liturgy will continue to occupy our concerns, especially regarding the power of liturgy to shape communal desire. It is the nature of liturgy to wholly engage the human person — body, intellect, desire, will, passions, memory, imagination — within the cultural context of the participants. It is necessary that all of these dimensions be engaged in making the links between liturgy and justice. Since liturgical forms are not just expressive but exploratory, critical and noetic, it will be interesting to see what new insights emerge about justice when all the dimensions of the human person are more fully engaged.

I see visual, poetic, musical and dramatic artists playing a more important role in keeping the connections alive. While song lyricists have increasingly lent their hand to the task, we need more non-textually based artists to startle our imaginations, to move our hearts, and to give voice and vision to our insights or even our disillusionment. These creative persons need to be given more space to mediate between groups, to speak the unspeakable, to create symbols for us to think about and, perhaps, to be the prophetic "thorn in our sides."

Finally, I see the need to develop a new understanding of the public character of worship. The church's unfolding understanding of its public responsibility to, for and in the world community as well as to, for and in the earth and cosmos will also have an impact on our understanding of worship as a public work. At least for the moment, we need liturgical forms and images that account for our preoccupation with difference and diversity even as we struggle for unity and common ground. Perhaps it is not incidental that issues of justice have become so pressing at a time when we are painfully realizing that universal claims to a common humanity tell only half the story. Our life experience is deeply shaped by significant differences in access to a healthy environment, to power, to food, to peace, or by economic, racial, class and gender distinctions. The church and its liturgy needs to add its voice to the conversation and struggle to find a way toward just living as differences threaten to overwhelm any sense of a shared humanity.

1. For our interest, see the following works: Paul Marx, *Virgil Michel and the Liturgical Movement* (Collegeville: Liturgical Press, 1957); R.W. Franklin, "Virgil Michel: An Introduction," *Worship* 62 (1988): 194–201; Kenneth R. Himes, "Eucharist and Justice: Assessing the Legacy of Virgil Michel," *Worship* 62 (1988): 201–224. See also the papers of the 1988 Virgil Michel Symposium, *The Future of the Catholic Church in America* (Collegeville: Liturgical Press, 1991), esp. articles by Mary Collins and Mark Searle.

2. Virgil Michel, "Liturgy and the Changing World," *Orate Fratres* 12 (1937): 1–7.

3. See the very helpful text *The Reception of Vatican II*, ed. G. Alberigo, J.-P. Jossua, and J. Komonchak (Washington, DC: Catholic University of America Press, 1987), especially articles by Segundo Galilea and Gustavo Guitierrez.

4. See, for example, the extensive bibliography at the end of *Liturgy, Justice and the Reign of God: Integrating Vision and Practice,* ed. F. Henderson, S. Larson and K. Quinn (New York: Paulist Press, 1989).

5. Elisabeth Schüssler Fiorenza, "Tablesharing and the Celebration of the Eucharist," *Can We Always Celebrate the Eucharist?* ed. M. Collins and D. Power, *Concilium* 152 (New York: Seabury Press, 1982): 3–12.

6. Marjorie Procter-Smith, *In Her Own Rite: Constructing Feminist Liturgical Tradition* (Nashville: Abingdon Press, 1990): 13.

7. Enrique Dussel, "The Bread of the Eucharistic Celebration as a Sign of Justice in the Community," in *Can We Always Celebrate the Eucharist?* p. 56–65.

8. Mary Collins, "Eucharist and Justice," in *Worship: Renewal to Practice* (Washington, D.C.: Pastoral Press, 1990): 247–263.

9. See also Kathleen Hughes, "Liturgy and Justice: An Intrinsic Relationship," in *Living No Longer For Ourselves: Liturgy and Justice in the Nineties,* ed. Kathleen Hughes and Mark Francis (Collegeville: Liturgical Press, 1991): 36–51.

10. Catherine Vincie, "Eucharist and the Cry for Justice," *Worship* 68 (1994): 194–212.

11. Mark Searle, "Private Religion, Individualistic Society, Common Worship," in *Liturgy and Spirituality in Context: Perspectives on Prayer and Culture,* ed. Eleanor Bernstein (Collegeville: Liturgical Press, 1990): 38–45.

12. Catherine Vincie, "Liturgical Assembly, Just Community, and the Role of the Catechist," *Liturgical Ministry* 3 (Spring 1994): 52–57.

13. Kenneth Himes, "Eucharist and Justice," *Worship* 62 (1988): 214.

Healing Society through Apostolic Preaching

Preaching in Today's World

"Yes, the days are coming, says the Lord God, when I will send famine upon the land: not a famine of bread, or thirst for water, but for hearing the Word of the Lord" (Amos 8:11). Although these words were written at least seven centuries before the birth of Christ, the message remains true today, throughout our country and throughout our world. While we lament the strong negative characteristics of our contemporary culture — exaggerated individualism, the divorce of faith from daily life, violence in the home, in neighborhoods, in our own hearts — we recognize at the same time some very positive aspects: a hunger for God, prayer and spirituality; a hunger for community; a search for meaning in our lives.

People are starving to hear the Word of God! They want to hear about Jesus Christ and are willing to gather anywhere to do so. People come together in many different locations with the preaching team to which I belong: in parking lots, in baseball fields, front and back lawns, carports, empty lots, beauty shops, city parks and gazebos, parish halls and churches. This tells us something about the need to expand our notion of preaching beyond the church building and the pulpit. There are, in fact, many ways in which and many places where we are called to break open the Word of God with the people and with one another.

The Incarnational Preaching of Jesus

Jesus was a very ordinary person who inserted himself in the midst of the life of the people where he was raised: "He pitched his tent among us" (John 1:14). He spent the first thirty years without many people knowing that he was called to a special ministry. When he entered into the more public time of his ministry, he shared from the life of the people, using the stories, parables and images of the people. He spoke of the mustard seed, the reign of God, the yeast in the dough, the buried treasure, the sower and the seed, the prodigal son. He shared from *within* the life of the people and their environment. The episode with the Samaritan woman (John 4:1–42) is one such example of how Jesus, as a preacher and evangelist, inserted himself into the life of people. It is a wonderful story of how Jesus entered into the reality of someone he met and of how he and she went forth from there exchanged and evangelized. He engaged her in a dialogue, accepting her, allowing her to enter deeply into herself and into his love. Her life was changed radically forever. She became a preacher and evangelizer for her town.

This is the way Jesus preached on the hillsides, in the desert, walking along the road, and in the Jewish synagogues.

Apostles and Apostolic Preaching

After Jesus' death, resurrection and ascension, his apostles made Jesus Christ himself the center of their message. They invited people to come to know him the same way the Samaritan woman experienced him in their encounter. Their activities are recorded in the Acts of the Apostles. Apostolic preaching included some of the twelve: Paul, deacons like Stephen and Philip. There were also women like Lydia and Priscilla. They expected that signs and healings would accompany their preaching and that the people would be moved by the Holy Spirit to change their lives. They were invited to give their lives over to the living reality of Jesus Christ present in their midst and would look for others to support them living a new way of life in a community of believers.

Apostolic preaching was accompanied by signs of healing, signs of freedom and of conversion with a desire for community. As Saint Augustine said, "The apostles preached and churches were born." Apostolic preaching included (1) proclaiming the living presence of the resurrected Jesus, (2) signs, healings and the freedom that accompanied the preaching, (3) conversions in the way of life of the hearers, (4) new life in a community, (5) evangelizing others, (6) sharing responsibility and leadership, (7) continuing the mission of Jesus and (8) bringing the Spirit of God into the world.

We today are called to continue this apostolic preaching, to continue to invite people to know Jesus Christ as a living reality in their lives. We as preachers, evangelists, catechists and liturgists must come to know Jesus in such a deep and personal way that anyone who sees us, hears us and experiences us will come to know the person of Jesus. Preaching Jesus today, his love and faithfulness means presenting the kerygma in such a way that people are invited to move from a cultural faith to an explicit commitment to the person of Jesus Christ. This means that he becomes the most important person in our lives, influencing our values, our hopes and our attitudes.

Who is Jesus for you? Jesus asks us: "Who do *you* say that I am?" (Luke 9:18–22).

The preaching event today disposes people to experience God through preaching, ritual and testimonies. It invites the listeners to make a personal commitment to Jesus Christ, resulting in a conversion process and entering into a community of believers. The engagement with the Word of God involves not only the preacher, but also the participants who share the Word of God. The preaching event includes ritual, song and testimonies of people who are willing to share their faith stories and their understanding of Jesus as they continue their walk of faith. Preaching also invites people into a community. We are not called to be isolated believers in Jesus but to be part of a gathering, part of church, part of a believing community.

Where Are We Called to Preach Today?

We are challenged to preach wherever the people live and wherever they are willing to gather. This is an important consideration especially for women who struggle with the issue of preaching in a church. We can share and break open the Word wherever people are willing to gather to listen. In my twenty-five years of experience, I have seen people willing to gather in new places if we are willing to go there; instead of expecting them to come to us, we must go out to them.

Today we are called to be a missionary church, not a church of the corporate model. We need to be concerned about the people who are not part of our parishes and the Sunday envelope system. We need to be a church that visits the sick, the elderly and the people who have been unchurched for many years.

In the diocese of Brownsville, Texas, Bishop John J. Fitzpatrick lived a missionary vision. Invariably, in each of my conversations with him, he would ask about "the 60 percent" who were not being reached by the church. The 60 percent were those who lived in poor neighborhoods and underdeveloped areas, the cultural Catholics not connected to the church for many reasons: hurts, poverty, anger, not having a car or adequate clothing for coming to church and many other reasons. Keep going out to them! We are called to continually include the unlikely people who have fallen through the cracks of the systems.

We are invited to be a missionary church in all areas. Some of the places our team has preached are a gazebo in a plaza; a front yard in Sanford, Colorado, where they had no church; in a carport in the inner city in San Antonio; in a baseball field in Goodyear, Arizona, where the neighborhood was isolated from the parish church; in front of the church; in parish parking lots; in a park on a lake for an afternoon picnic that included prayer and preaching.

Who is Hungry for the Word Today?

Many people are starving for God in their lives. Hunger exists among the young, prisoners, depressed peoples, the middle class, the aged in nursing homes, in inner cities, single parents, those who are divorced, the widowed, and the elderly. It is important, no matter our living circumstances, to look for the poor. There are poor living even in the most affluent areas. People who seem affluent can be struggling for food and clothing, trying to make payments on their elegant homes.

We need to remember that Jesus was always concerned for the poor. "Blessed are the poor for the kingdom of heaven is theirs" (Matthew 5:3). As Gustavo Gutierrez has written, "History, where God reveals himself and where we proclaim him, must be reread from the side of the poor." The presence of God among them is crystal clear because they know their true needs.

Related to this subject of *where* we are called to preach is inculturation, an issue that has become increasingly important in the post–Vatican II church. Inculturation is not just a consideration for those working with Hispanics, Haitians, Asians and African Americans. Regardless of whether we live in the suburbs or in the inner city, Maine, south Texas or Africa, we are being challenged as preachers to proclaim the word of God as Jesus did and to enter into the reality of the life, the stories and the experiences of the people with whom we minister. What we say must connect with their lives so that the faith life we are talking about may penetrate the values of their daily lives. We preach from within the life experiences of the people and proclaim the presence of Jesus within their world. It is important that we become inculturated and that we understand the people's lives and struggles. As M. Catherine Hilkert has written, preaching is "naming the action of God within the context of peoples' lives."

We need to meditate on the stories and images of the people we work with. What is the culture, history and language of those with whom we minister? We need to enter into the customs and popular religiosity of the people to make connections with the word of God. In my ministry with Hispanics, for example, it is important to understand the significance of Our Lady of Guadalupe.

Who is Sent to Preach?

Who is sent to preach? "Someone who knows they have been entrusted with God's word for others: someone who is driven to speak the word of truth, love, mercy and justice which they have received from God in Jesus Christ" (Mary O'Driscoll).

Every one of us who has been baptized is entrusted with a message to share with others and is called to be an evangelist, a missionary. As with Jesus, so our mission also is twofold: Jesus announced and proclaimed the loving compassion of his Father and accompanied that with signs of healing, liberation and peace. We too are called to announce the living reality of Jesus and can expect signs of his power, love and forgiveness in our lives.

Jesus, however, did not minister alone; he formed a community of ministers including women. He worked in what we would call today a "collaborative model." For 23 years I have preached as part of a team of priests, religious men and women, and laity. We invite couples, single parents and young people, including children, to share their faith stories. (A seven-year-old girl volunteered in a retreat to share her story.) As ministers, we listen to the faith story of others to accompany them as they share their experiences. As we listen, their sense of personal dignity deepens and they are empowered to share that story with others, whether it be in a small community, a support group or a nursing home. Their witnessing enables them to become preachers.

As baptized people who share in the ministry of Jesus and the priesthood of the people, we look for ways to draw people into ministry. Lay people today are manifesting a passion for ministry. Each person brings a unique faith perspective. A mother has a faith experience that others do not, and the widowed can relate their story. Together, our faith experiences enrich the presentation of the gospel and open others to telling their stories.

What Happens in the Preaching Event?

What happens as we are proclaiming the word of God? There are two aspects: affective changes and effective changes. Both happen simultaneously.

Affective preaching means that as the word is spoken, people are moved in their hearts to a love of God, to praise, to an awareness of the need for forgiveness or simply an awareness of goodness. The movement of our bodies, our hands, our voices, our eyes, our smile, the way we share the word of God, becomes important. It moves people to a trust, to a sense of community, to the courage to make some decision.

Preaching is also *effective* in that we expect God to accompany us, both preacher and listeners. Preaching is a dynamic engagement with the people and with God's active presence in the listeners, bringing about effective changes. We need to expect changes in people's lives.

The primary effect of the word of God in our lives is that we discover our dignity as persons, as true sons and daughters of God. As we grow in acknowledging this dignity, we begin to recognize that same dignity in our brothers and sisters, husbands, wives and children. Many of our brothers and sisters have been martyred in Central and South America, South Africa and other parts of the world as a consequence of having discovered anew in the word of God their own dignity and that of others.

The primary effect of the small faith communities is that people are growing in the awareness of their true dignity. One of the cries we hear in our churches is the need for motivation, the need to find a way to encourage more catechists, readers and choir members. As people grow in excitement and are driven to share their experience of Jesus, they will be willing to enter ministry. We must accompany them through their stages of growth, first sharing their personal story, then sharing it in a small group and finally in a large group. This is the ministry of accompanying and empowering others.

We can expect and have seen marvelous changes in the family, especially in the area of communication and returning to family prayer. Families are making great sacrifices to have time for personal meditation and prayer together. Through the custom of family forgiveness sessions, there is a rediscovery of the gifts families have to give to one another. Parents are called to be pastors of the faith to their families, aware that this is their vocation with their children. These are some of the changes that come from the word of God as families take time together.

People are meeting in small faith communities, 12-step groups and RCIA groups in their neighborhoods. As they meet in their homes, other neighbors know what is happening. This is the beginning of healing the bonds among neighbors. Trust, confidence and unity begin to emerge anew as people are brought out of their unhappy isolation and begin to reach out to others in the same area.

Through the presence of such groups, violence has diminished in some inner-city areas. In San Antonio, Texas, for example, a small group of elderly women decided to let go of their paralyzing fear. They began to spend time on their front porches, walk the streets at night and greet the gangs along the way. Many of the gang members were sons and daughters of their neighbors. Gradually they inspired others to do the same. The diminishing of violence is often what happens when persons come to know and trust each other.

The effects of the word of God also carry over into the workplace. An occupation or profession is no longer simply a way to earn a living; a sense of mission begins to emerge. Our work is a contribution with others to the broader society. Understanding work in new ways leads to seeing new ways to promote better relationships in the workplace.

As we share the word of God in our families and in the groups that we minister with, values come to the fore that are very much at the heart of the mission of social justice: the value of community vs. individualism, the value of solidarity vs. divisiveness, the value of collaboration vs. competition, the value of respecting the individual, the woman and her gifts, the man and his gifts, the elderly and the mission they still have, the young and their hopes. These are values that are at the heart of what it means to be men and women of justice and values that permeate the gospel.

The word of God entrusted to us is not isolated from our daily lives and struggles, the inner cities and depressed areas, the loneliness in nursing homes, the uneasiness in affluent areas. The word of God is enmeshed in these real life situations. We need to weave together our daily lives and our faith lives through breaking open the word.

Small Faith Communities as Seeds of Hope

Many small communities are springing up throughout the country and throughout the world. They are functioning in many different ways. Various movements in the church — such as Charismatic Renewal, Cursillos, Catholic Family Movement, Marriage Encounter and Renew — have as their common purpose to continue that faith experience in small groups. These groups come together to pray, to break open the word of God and to share their faith journey. As they continue to meet weekly, the people become bonded together in a new way of loving, a new way of respecting and a new way of seeing both their own lives and those of the people around them. This, then, empowers them to reach out to others in ministry. People are enabled to be communion ministers for the homebound in their neighborhoods, to visit prisons and to get involved in neighborhood organizations. The unity within the small group gives them the courage and energy to reach out beyond themselves.

Such small communities are planting seeds for the transformation of society. Small communities are also seen as the hope and future of our church, our country and the world. My sixteen years of experience of the small communities in the diocese of Brownsville has shown me the power and promise of the word of God in the midst of the people. A dramatic transformation has taken place in

Helen Marie Raycraft, op

one of the poorest areas of the country. At least 500 small communities have been meeting weekly under their own leadership. Some parishes have a network of 30 to 40 communities. They have brought new creative life to the church with an excitement in sharing the mission of Jesus today. More than 1200 people were trained in lay ministry, 80 percent of whose energy and motivation came from participation in small faith communities. The small communities are truly seeds of transformation and hope for the church and society.

"This is God's dwelling place among people. He shall dwell with them and shall be their God who is always with them. He shall wipe every tear from their eyes, and there shall be no death or mourning, crying out or pain, for the former world has passed away" (Revelation 21:3 – 4).

Julia Upton, RSM

Personal Obstacles to Ritual Prayer

In this essay, I present seven personal "obstacles" to ritual prayer that challenge us today. The obstacles are real for all of us, but their size, shape and configuration will be different for each person: Some will be small inconveniences, others monumental blockades. Those who are graceful may be able to leap over one obstacle with a grand jete, while another, less graceful, will stumble and fall.

Learned Disabilities

The first obstacle I label "learned disabilities." Surely you are familiar with the broad category of "learning disabilities," which are generally considered to be either congenital or the result of accidents during birth. "Learned disabilities" are not congenital; we are born without them but gradually become dis-abled as we grow and mature.

The inability to listen, for example, is one of these "learned disabilities." This may be one of the unfortunate by-products of technology, particularly in cities, where there is an increasing amount of noise that we need to tune out if we are to keep our sanity. We do not naturally tune things out; the ability to do so is something that one develops gradually. Infants and young children tune in to everything, especially what you don't want them to hear. They approach all of life with openness and eagerness, but somewhere along the way we choose not to be so attentive. What has happened to us?

At the Sunday assembly, this "learned disability" affects our ability to listen during the liturgy of the word. The first word in the Rule of Saint Benedict is "Listen!" I find myself wanting to begin the liturgy of the word with that command each Sunday. Many people in the congregation presume that the prayers are the same week in and week out. They are deaf to the nuance of themes. Missalettes, sound systems and poor lectors aside, very few people are willing or able to listen to the word of God or for the voice of God, either in ritual prayer or in their everyday lives.

Despite our valiant efforts to get people to put down the missalette, they would rather read along. I can, of course, understand the need for those who have difficulty hearing, but for others I wonder if it isn't just a habit forged in the days when the liturgy was in Latin and we followed along as best we could in our missals. Or it might be the need to control, not to be caught off guard. Being read to does put one into a state of dependency, bringing us back at least unconsciously to the time when we were not yet able to read.

It is said that 95 percent of what we learn is apprehended through our sense of sight, so people might have learned to trust their sense of sight more than their sense of hearing. The goal of the liturgy of the word, however, is not to learn or study the sacred texts but to let them wash over us again and again, with different aspects sinking in each time. Perhaps we haven't been clear enough about this in preparing people for celebrating the liturgy.

Lack of Spontaneity

The second learned disability is lack of spontaneity, or as Doris Donnelly put it in her January 1992 *Worship* article, an inability to praise.[1] Again, just look to the children at Sunday worship. The celebrant assumes the *orans* position, and so do the children in the first row. They seem to have a natural sense of ritual and play that along the way to adulthood is unlearned. They throw their whole being into what they are doing, losing all sense of time, personal problems and emotional distance as they abandon themselves to the moment.

While I am the first to applaud and encourage "full, conscious, active participation by all the faithful" and rejoice that the *Constitution on the Sacred Liturgy* insists that this participation is "the aim to be considered before all else,"[2] it has also been proven to have a shadow side for many of the faithful. This is the second obstacle I see: Ritual abuse. In calling it this, I am not speaking about abuse of the ritual but abuse by the ritual. And there are many examples of this in our rites. Few in my diocese will forget the Chrism Mass where, following an elaborate gospel procession and incensation of the book of the gospels, and a fine proclamation of the gospel pericope, the deacon held up a missalette, chanting "This is the gospel of the Lord." Such liturgical atrocities happen more often than we might like to think.[3]

Another area of concern within the sphere of this obstacle is the role of women in the liturgy. Don't we women come to celebrate eucharist as baptized Christians, as equal members of the Christian community, to share in the Lord's banquet? Yet the whole topic of "the role of women in the liturgy" presupposes that a woman's role at the eucharist is somehow different from that of a man. Because of this, it seems that women indeed have no role in the liturgy — except by way of exception.[4] Liturgical law and liturgical language make it clear that women are not as welcome as we might think. As women become more aware of this form of ritual abuse, it becomes a deeply personal obstacle to ritual prayer.

Adversarialism

The third obstacle is a behavior pattern observable in many social relations — in the home, in the workplace and even at worship.

This is "adversarialism," a kind of "them versus us" mentality.[5] In different contexts, two influential "churchmen" have recently expressed observations of adversarialism in the church. In recent interviews, Cardinal Ratzinger attributes adversarialism to the altar having been turned around to face the people.[6] And Ladislaus Orsy, SJ, in an address to the National Association of Diocesan Ecumenical Officers, noted that never before the promulgation of the new *Code of Canon Law* in 1983 had "there been such a sharp line drawn between clergy and laity."[7] My own recent conversation with a group of people from the "thirtysomething" generation has led me to conclude that adversarialism can also be caused by disillusionment. Raised in the days of the first flush of conciliar reform, many people now raising young children thought that by this time in their lives they would have a stronger voice and a greater role in church ministry.

Adversarialism is detected in many different ways, especially in "priest-bashing," but one somewhat more subtle way in which this obstacle becomes evident is in what psychologists term "hypermnesia."[8] This is the opposite of amnesia (forgetting everything) and is characterized by an individual remembering everything, even the most insignificant details. It is the result of an unconscious hypervigilance in which one is constantly on the outlook for a word, a phrase, an attitude, a pattern that the adversary might use. Psychologists see this type of behavior most often in people who have been severely abused as children,[9] but I think we can see its parallel operative in the church when one word or phrase will set up an immediate blockade to a person's hearing or participating in the liturgy.

Addiction

"Addiction" is the fourth personal obstacle to ritual prayer. Many psychologists and theologians today are involved in studies of addiction.[10] Addiction has been defined as any mood-altering substance or process to which one has surrendered oneself.[11] Addictions take control of us and cause us to do and think things that are inconsistent with our values, evidenced by a sudden need to deceive ourselves and others. The list which was once limited to alcohol, nicotine and narcotics has now been expanded to include work, sex, sports, gambling, exercise, worry and religion — that is, religion of the "quick-fix" variety that does not include thoughtful prayer or meditation. Addiction furthermore is both founded on and fueled by denial.

In the liturgy, we come upon some people who are addicted to a romantic past that never existed. They long for the days of the "beautiful Latin mass, when liturgy was always uplifting," and it seems that nothing we do now is acceptable.

Others are addicted to busyness in its many forms. The most obvious effect of this addiction on worship, it would seem, is that it creates the illusion that one doesn't have time for ritual prayer. People absent themselves from the Sunday assembly because they have been out late the night before and need their rest, because their children have Little League, or because Sunday is the only day they can get the shopping, laundry or yard work done. Liturgy requires leisure, and if one is addicted to work or business, one never has leisure.[12]

What Rollo May refers to as "the seduction of the new"[13] and Neil Postman calls "our boundless lust for what is new"[14] is basically consumerism, the addiction to consumption. People who are addicted in this way are not able to become rooted, and they find repetition itself boring. They have no felt connection to things, no appreciation for symbols or rituals. "The homelessness we see on our city streets," psychologist Thomas Moore writes, "is a reflection of a deeper homelessness we feel in our hearts."[15]

To be addicted is to have sold your soul. "To elevate one god," Neil Postman writes in his book *Technopoly,* "requires the demotion of another. 'Thou shalt have no other gods before me' applies as well to a technological divinity as any other."[16] The issue, therefore, is not that the liturgy just isn't what it used to be, or that one does not have time for ritual prayer, or that liturgy is boring, but rather that the worship of different gods requires different rituals. When one renders to Caesar the things that are God's, one can't then render them to God.

No Fasting Before Worship

The fifth personal obstacle to ritual prayer is that we no longer fast before coming to worship. I do not mean just fasting from food but rather hungering both physically and spiritually. I received first communion in the days when we fasted from midnight on, and from everything. Even when the fast laws changed in 1952, 1957 and again in 1964, I remember how we checked our watches before getting in the communion line.

First, it was never clear whether the hour of fasting was before the time Mass began or communion, so we timed it with communion. There we sat in the pew, waiting for the required hour to elapse. If time fell short of that hour, we waited for the end of the line, and if we were still short, we didn't receive communion that day.

I am not suggesting a return to those often "mindless" practices. There is something, however, to be said for coming to the banquet table hungry.

Perhaps you know the story of the young man who eagerly came to the famous Zen master seeking enlightenment. The teacher began their session by pouring the young man a cup of tea. The master did not stop pouring when the cup was full, however, but kept pouring and pouring. Certain that his teacher had become distracted, the student said, "Master, the cup is overflowing!"

"So are you, my friend," he answered. "I cannot teach you anything, for you are too full of your own ideas. Go away and do not return until you are empty."

I cannot think of anything but physical hunger that can remind us ultimately of our deep spiritual hunger for communion with each other and with God.

We also need to be "emptied" of our own ideas of how things ought to be. My brother-in-law was the general manager of Avery Fisher Hall at Lincoln Center in New York. Although he could have had house seats to any Broadway play on any night of the week, he never went to the theater. He told me it was because he would be so distracted by the conditions of the theater itself that he would never be able to enjoy the play. If he had only learned to fast from such concerns, he might have had some great nights at the theater. Now, I trust that Bob is no longer distracted by such concerns but feasting on "rich food and well-aged wines"[17] at the eternal banquet table. But while he walked this earth, he taught me to fast — to come to the banquet table hungry and to leave room for dessert.

Unrealistic Expectations

The sixth is an enormous obstacle, that of "unrealistic expectations," a by-product, I believe, of having sold our souls to the entertainment industry. Surely you have heard people excuse themselves from the common table week after week because they "don't get anything out of it." One way I translate that is, "It isn't entertaining enough." In substantiating his diagnosis that we Americans are "amusing ourselves to death," Neil Postman observes that all public discourse — politics, religion, news, athletics, education and commerce — has gradually taken on the form of entertainment, "transformed into congenial adjuncts of show business."[18]

I see that most obviously when I turn on the evening news on commercial television. Little of real substance is ever presented these days, and what little one does find is never developed. We are fed sound-bites of significance and pseudo-significance, titillated but not informed.

"Entertainment" is defined as "a performance intended to amuse or divert," the exact opposite of ritual prayer, which is intended to focus and re-direct us. No wonder there is so much personal disillusionment with the liturgy: It puts too many demands on us in a world that increasingly requires less and less. We expect upbeat music, relevant homilies and a service that makes us feel good.

The homily, it seems, has become the new focal point of the liturgy, both for presiders and the assembly. A lot of time, energy and attention goes into the homily, and that is good; but it must be clearly seen as part of the fabric of prayer and not as a free-standing routine.

The same is true of the music. The purpose of weaving music into the liturgy is to move us to prayer, and that is a delicate balance in the entertainment age.

The Covert Contract

The seventh, and last obstacle might be the largest single obstacle to ritual prayer: the "covert" contract (often made on our behalf at infant baptism) into meanings and even behaviors that we didn't choose. Let me explain what I mean by way of an analogy to marriage. In the overt contract in marriage, the vows exchanged are:

> I promise to be true to you in good times and in bad, in sickness and in health. I will love you and honor you all the days of my life.[19]

The covert contract is what is not said but what is secretly intended. Such a contract might really mean: "In good times and in health," or "for security and pleasure," or "for happily ever after" or "until it becomes inconvenient."

With baptism there are the overt contracts, those things explicitly expressed in the rite celebrated, like baptism into the death and resurrection of the Lord Jesus, as Paul tells is in his Letter to the Romans (6:3 – 8). But there is also the "package" that goes along with initiation, our incorporation into the culture of a Catholic community. Some people put on merely the veneer of Christianity; others put on the humbled, abandoned Christ, taking him into every fiber of their being.

A striking example of the attraction to the "veneer" appeared in the July 1993 issue of *Vogue* magazine. Underneath a full page of glittering designer crosses ranging up to $6,250 in price, there is a paragraph on the challenge of designing crosses. Admitting that the problem is that crosses have so many different meanings for people, artist/designer Maria Snyder concludes that "a cross symbolizes love." The copy reads

> Both as streetwise pendants and as couture pieces, crosses have had a popular revival in recent months, and looking

ahead to fall, with medieval-inspired fashion making its mark,
a cross worn at the neck or pinned to a jacket will continue to
be the definitive accessory of the moment.[20]

For someone who has put on the veneer (or fashion accessory) of
Christianity, ritual prayer is equally peripheral, but for someone
who has put on the whole Christ and who sees the eyes of Christ in
every face, ritual prayer is central.

Conclusion

That completes the list of what I consider to be significant personal
obstacles to ritual prayer, but let me add a word of caution about
these and any of the obstacles we happen upon in the spiritual life.
None, I believe, is totally insurmountable, although each, depending on its size and substance, will demand a different approach
once we realize it is there. And that is the key: acknowledging that
the obstacle is there.

An undergraduate taught me something very important about
these obstacles about ten years ago. It was mid-semester and we
were beginning the unit on marriage in my undergraduate liturgy
course. I asked for a show of hands as to how many of them regularly attended Sunday worship. Three students out of the 60
enrolled in the course raised their hands. I then asked how many
would choose to celebrate their marriages in the Catholic church.
Every hand went up, and I registered surprise, asking for their reasons. This, as you might expect, elicited the usual list of responses:
"The church is beautiful"; "I love the long aisle"; "I always
dreamed it would be like that"; "My parents want it that way";
"I'm Catholic." The list ran on until I came to a young woman
seated in the front row. When I asked her why she would want to
celebrate the sacrament of marriage when she never celebrates the
sacrament of eucharist, her whole facial expression changed and
her eyes came to life as she said, amazing even herself, "I guess I
really believe!"

We never know what it will be that awakens us or others to
the obstacles that have found their way into our lives. We need to

be as patient with each other as Jesus was with his disciples, and to surrender ourselves, in the words of the poet John Shea,

> to a mystery which masks itself
>   as a mistake
> and a power which perfects itself
>   in weakness.[21]

1. Doris Donnelly, "Impediments to Praise in the Worshiping Community," *Worship* 66 (January 1992): 39–53. In this article the author proposes five impediments to praise: a lack of affirmation in our personal lives; the absence of community; a suspicion of the emotions; an inability to live with conflict; and self-groundedness.

2. *Sacrosanctum Concilium*, 14.

3. See Aidan Kavanagh, *Elements of Rite: A Handbook of Liturgical Style* (New York: Pueblo, 1982), and Dennis Smolarski, *How Not To Say Mass* (New York: Paulist, 1986).

4. See *Appendix to the General Instruction of the Roman Missal for the Dioceses of the United States of America*, 66.

5. "Adversarialism" frames the discussion for M. Scott Peck, M.D., *A World Waiting to be Born: Civility Rediscovered* (New York: Bantam, 1993), which gives us some helpful ways of addressing this obstacle both individually and communally.

6. Robert Moynihan, "Ratzinger Prefers Altar Turned Around Again," *National Catholic Reporter* (May 28, 1993): 7.

7. Ladislaus Orsy, SJ, "'Kenosis': The Door to Christian Unity," *Origins* 23 (June 3, 1993): 39.

8. For a more complete discussion of this see John Bradshaw, *Creating Love: The Next Great Stage of Growth* (New York: Bantam, 1992): 75.

9. See the *Diagnostic and Statistical Manual* (DSM)-IV.

10. See Patrick McCormick, *Sin As Addiction* (New York: Paulist Press, 1989): 146, 161.

11. For a complete discussion of this subject see Anne Wilson Schaef, *Beyond Therapy, Beyond Science: A New Model for Healing the Whole Person* (San Francisco: HarperCollins, 1992); *When Society Becomes an Addict* (San Francisco: Harper & Row, 1987); *The Addictive Organization*, written with Diane Fassel (San Francisco: Harper & Row, 1988).

12. See Juliet B. Shor, *The Overworked American: The Unexpected Decline of Leisure* (New York: Basic Books, 1991).

13. Rollo May, *The Cry for Myth* (New York: Norton, 1991): 101.

14. Neil Postman, *Technopoly: The Surrender of Culture to Technology* (New York: Random House, 1992): 11.

15. Thomas Moore, *Care of the Soul: A Guide for Cultivating Depth and Sacredness in Everyday Life* (San Francisco: HarperCollins, 1992): 271.

16. Postman, *Technopoly,* p. 165.

17. Isaiah 25:6.

18. Neil Postman, *Amusing Ourselves to Death: Public Discourse in the Age of Show Business* (NY: Penguin, 1985): 3–4.

19. Rite of Marriage, no. 25.

20. "Vogue's Last Look," *Vogue* (June 1993): 238.

21. John Shea, "The Prayer of the Holy Sacrifice of the Mass," *The Hour of the Unexpected* (Allen, Texas: Argus, 1977): 77.

Born of the Spirit!

> The wind blows where it chooses; you hear the sound of it,
> but you do not know where it comes from or where it is goes.
> So it is with everyone who is born of the Spirit. (John 3:8)

In short, with the Spirit of God "ain't nothing impossible!"

Sarah and Abraham were far too old.
Moses was a stammering shepherd.
Jeremiah was far too young.
Mary, by her own admission,
　　was but the handmaid of the Lord.
Peter and John had neither silver nor gold.
Paul attested that he had a thorn in the flesh.
Angelo Roncalli was from Bergamo —
a peasant, an old man, a caretaker pope
who would surely not rock the boat.
Martin Luther King Jr. was from Atlanta —
a young man, an assistant to his "Daddy,"
who would most certainly
do nothing more than deliver erudite sermons
about the Promised Land to come in that great by and by.
And Jesus? — a carpenter, a son and a brother and a neighbor!
How is it that such miraculous deeds

were accomplished by their hands?
How indeed!

Might it be because God's Spirit blows where it wills?
Might it be because our God is indeed a God of power and
  might?
Yes, our God works wonders.
Our God is not limited by our limited nature.
In the power of the Spirit from above
our God can do the extraordinary in the ordinary.

That old, laughing couple produced the very hope of Israel
from whom sprang a race
more numerous than the sands along the sea shore.
That stammerer stretched out his arm
and led a people through the Red Sea dry-shod.
That kid thundered God's name, blasted a people,
and gave them sure hope of a better day.
That handmaid did say "Yes"
and from her God-bearing womb burst forth
  the Sun of Justice.
Those two apostles had the name of Jesus
and empowered a man to leap for joy.
That barbed one pricked our conscience.
That portly pope engendered *aggiornamento*.
That Southern Baptist preacher initiated a movement.
And that crucified carpenter cured the sick,
raised the dead, cleansed lepers, and cast out demons.

Are you with me?
An elderly couple, a stutterer, a boy-child, a teenage girl,
two disciples on their own, an "arrogant" fanatic, a peasant,
a "colored" preacher, and an itinerant craftsman —
God can effect such wonders in the lives of such simple folk.
Might it be because our God is beyond our comprehending?

For my thoughts are not your thoughts,
  nor are your ways my ways,
    says the Lord. (Isaiah 55:8)

J-Glenn Murray, SJ

There is some startling news: What God has done in the past,
God is willing, waiting, and wanting to do in the present.
God longs to do marvelous deeds today.
And God does.
The Spirit of God is still blowing where it wills.
In a simple conversation around the kitchen table
when a hardened and seasoned bigot
might come to see that women, and Blacks,
and anyone not of our class or theological persuasion
are heirs to the one and same reign of God—
that equal opportunity, housing, a warm bed,
a nourishing meal, and safety are their birthright in God,
then in that conversation the demon racism is cast out.
And the Spirit of the risen Lord is at work!

In a hospital room when a hollow-eyed,
lesioned AIDS patient gains strength to cry
not only in pain but in thanksgiving,
then those who are far too often labeled lepers are cleansed.
And the Spirit of the risen Lord is at work!

In a rectory parlor or counseling room
when a husband and wife engaged in bloody warfare
based on lame excuses
and limp accusations might come to walk together
toward a possible future of trust and sure-footed hope,
then a dead marriage is raised to new life.
And the Spirit of the risen Lord is at work!

At the Sunday eucharist when our sin-sick,
impoverished assemblies might hear a song to lift them up,
might hear a word to get them through,
might taste and see the how good God is,
then our sin-sick souls are made sanguine
and we are made whole.
Truly, the Spirit of the risen Lord is at work!

The sick still long for cure,
the dead still yearn to be raised,
the lepers still hope for cleansing,
and God knows

Born of the Spirit!

that legion is still the name of the demons among us.
And what extraordinary things God has done in the past,
God does today!

Well, here we are, ordinary folk gathered in,
some old and others older,
a variety of hues and classes, women and men,
rich and poor —
ordinary — all. Yes?

Well, ordinary people,
Please remember this: God alone performs wonders.
Get ready to be set on your feet.
Get ready for the room of your soul to shake and rock.
For the Spirit of the risen Lord has already been given to you.

Come, O Holy Spirit
O nameless treasure of the poor
O unfading hope of the oppressed
O touch of tender mercy
Come, O Mother of endless embrace
O Beloved Name that moves us to dance
O healing of the hardened heart
O sweet smoke that fills the temple.
Come, O pillar of fire that blazes our way.
Come, O freedom of the enslaved.
Come, O fragrant anointing of God's holy people.
Come, O Holy Spirit, O Love, O Light, O Life.[1]

Come, Holy Spirit, and rock this place
that we and all might know
that our God, who works wonders,
 is not through with us yet!

1. The "Invocation of the Holy Spirit" is copyright © 1995 by Richard
Edward McCarron and is based on the "Mystical Hymn of the Holy Spirit" by
Simeon the New Theologian. Used with permission.

Pope John XXIII:
A Loving Shepherd

Homily on the following readings: 2 Corinthians 11:1–11 and Matthew 6:7–15

The person to whom we owe thanks for the renewal of the liturgy in Vatican II is Angelo Roncalli, who on October 28, 1958, became Pope John XXIII for the second time. The first one to take the same name and the same number was Baldassare Cossa, an antipope of the great schism, who claimed the title from 1410–1415.

Just after John XXIII was elected, I received a postcard from an Italian priest at the Vatican with the cryptic note: *Il nuovo Papa é molto amabile, umile, abile, pastorale, pratico e semplice, e gli piace muoversi:* "The new Pope is very kind, humble, capable, pastoral, practical and simple; and he likes to move around."

The reading from 2 Corinthians in today's eucharist points to Paul's difficulties with the community at Corinth. "I wish you would bear with me," he says. "I may be untrained in speech, but not in knowledge," and "God knows I love you." How Paul would have liked to hear my friend's description of John XXIII used to describe his ministry at Corinth. The only part the Corinthians would apply to him, it seems, is the last phrase: "He likes to move around." In fact, after Paul had made an attempt at ministry in

Corinth, some of them came to him and said: "Paul, they really need you at Ephesus!"

John XXIII was a loving shepherd. That was so evident on October 11, 1962, the day of the opening of Vatican II. On the evening of that day, tired as he was and determined to make the opening ceremony the sole event, he gave in to the crowd that gathered in Saint Peter's Square and came to his window to talk to them in a very simple and affectionate way. He closed by saying: "Now you mothers and fathers who are here, go home and give your children a hug, and tell them it is from the Pope." His opening speech at the council was filled with human understanding and concern — a pastoral council, no condemnations, no prophets of doom: "the substance of the ancient doctrine of the deposit of faith is one thing, the way in which it is presented is another." Openness, consideration, ecumenical concerns — all these things which he emphasized had been already amply demonstrated by his life as a bishop.

He was the weak and foolish one chosen by God to confound the wise and the strong. John XXIII demonstrated his strength, his wisdom and his pastoral love in many ways. All the experiences came together in the council. And yet he was not immediately or universally accepted. He and the council fathers who were sensitive to his vision and plans for the church were criticized and condemned by others who claimed thereby to be the "super apostles."

John and the council were trying to renew the church, to present her once again as a spotless bride to Christ. Paul considered himself the father of the Corinthian church, so he was doing what fathers of that time and that culture did. He was arranging the marriage for the church in Corinth — his daughter in Christ — the marriage between God and the assembled people of God.

We are heirs to the same process. We are called by our baptism to continue the same activity. Our responsibility is to the local church which claims us as members, to see that church as a bride of Christ and to give her the gift that every bride needs most — love! We are committed to work together to prepare the wedding feast.

According to Luke's account of the Lord's prayer, the apostles had had a marvelous experience of unity in prayer. They wanted to be able to repeat this, to bring it back again, so they came with the request, "Lord, teach us to pray." It was then that Jesus gave them the prayer. We say that prayer at the crucial moment in our liturgical celebration when Christ is presented in the accomplishments of his paschal mystery and we are about to celebrate the banquet of the wedding of the Lamb.

In the eucharist we contemplate Christ in glory, giving all praise to the Creator in the unity of the Holy Spirit, and then we say the family prayer that involves all Christians — the prayer that makes us truly sisters and brothers in Christ — gathered in peace to celebrate the marriage between God and the assembly.

We lift our hands to God in heaven and then reach out to one another in the sign of peace, a symbol that tells us who we are and what our deepest responsibilities must be.

"Forgive us our sins as we forgive others," we pray. We really ask God to accept us when we ask pardon of others, because in offending them, we have offended God. Why do we as church people have so much trouble asking pardon for our individual and collective wrongs? Pope John, from the beginning of the council (especially in his ecumenical efforts but in other areas of church life as well), called for that kind of Christian action.

His openness to socialism and to the Orthodox, and his sensitivity to Judaism and the religions of the Middle East — all these things began or became effective realities with the council of Pope John. "Lovable, humble, pastoral, capable, simple." These qualities should describe the features on the face of the church whose marvelous mystical betrothal we celebrate in this eucharist. They will be seen on the face of the church only if they are evident in us. Corinth demanded a lot from Paul. Should our fellow Christians expect any less of you and me?

Gertrud Mueller Nelson

Things Lost
in Need of Finding:
A Homily for Evening Prayer

Welcome. Welcome into the twilight, that lingering threshold light "when shadows lengthen, evening comes, the busy world is hushed, the fever of life is over, and our work is done."

The liminal hours of twilight place us between the two great lights of sun and moon. It brings the favorite light of the impressionist painter — when the world turns achingly beautiful and some unnamed longing takes hold of the heart. So powerful and holy is twilight that indigenous people in many cultures stop everything to address the shadows now electric with spirits.

And just as the sun sets and before the night arrives, the Jewish mother lights the candles and ushers in the Sabbath as a bride. Those ceremonial candles shed a light on this world which is not the harsh light of the sun but a light gentle as wisdom, subtle as insight.

And isn't it so, that twilight brings a moment of fear as we see light "bending toward darkness"? Then our impulse is to gather together, and our deepest longing is like that of the disciples on the road to Emmaus: Lord, stay with us, for night approaches and the day is growing dim. We hook elbows, if you will. We pray. We per-

Gertrud Mueller Nelson

form our rites. We seek to bridge the gap between sun and moon, indeed, between heaven and earth. We long to experience, in our very blood and bone, God-with-us. We would be God's people, and God would be our God.

I've come to musing if twilight, on some level, might not also be the favorite light of the liturgist — aware, somehow, that too many experience our liminal moments not transfigured by grace but merely stuck in traffic. Anonymous and isolated from the surrounding masses, we sit, tinned up on the road going nowhere or sprung loose and set adrift from those ties which make our lives whole and organic.

Romano Guardini's concern, voiced in 1930, is still, painfully, on the mark: Humankind

> has fallen away on the one hand into a world of abstraction, on the other into the purely physical sphere; from union with nature into the purely scholastic and artificial; from the community into isolation. Our deepest longing should be to become once more one of the people; not indeed by romantic attempts to conform with popular ideas and customs, but by a renewal of our inmost spirit by a progressive return to a simple and complete life. (Romano Guardini, *The Church and the Catholic* and *The Spirit of the Liturgy*, trans. Ada Lane [New York: Sheed and Ward, 1935]: 20)

The liturgist knows that grace is real life. The liturgist sees that twilight casts a new light on everything that is at hand, everything that we have taken for granted, everything we have found too common to have worth, and in this new light, a right worth is returned them. Worth-ship is worship. Between the sun of intellectual analysis and the darkness of our being simply asleep to this world, these concrete, material objects, these simple gestures, this ancient story, all become transfused and transfigured. This stuff, redeemed by the mystery of God's flesh-taking, is the right stuff and worthy vehicle of the holy.

The kingdom of God is at hand, indeed, handy, accessible. The kingdom of God is among us: in bread and wine, in earth and ashes, in fire and water and oil and incense, in seeds and songs, in branches and bodies and babies, in signs and words and gestures.

This is the tangible stuff that belongs to us all and is the very ground of our being.

Cast in this light, liturgy is not the religion of an elite but the religion of the people because it cuts beyond abstract ideas and is simply up and doing what the human heart already knows. Liturgy returns us to community because if the saving power of God is to be manifest in each of us — in the graced reality of our lives — in the stuff of this earth, then our concerns must become communal, ecological, global. Liturgy is inclusive because in the realm of being and gesture, image and rites, there is a form for the practical and the profound, the hero and the mystic, the direct and earthy experience of mystery, and — though we have been perhaps too diligent in our efforts to eradicate it — there is allowed in liturgy something that borders on primal superstition. Gasp!

Let me tell you a story. Even as I was fretting my way into a fifth version of these reflections, the doorbell rang. Muttering over the interruption, I opened the door and was pleased to find our young friend the carpenter. Six weeks ago he'd come to this door to say good-bye. It was a last stop before leaving on a trip to visit his family in the swamplands of Texas. He had come to say good-bye and to ask a favor: First looking at his shoes and then glancing out the window, he said he'd heard from his friend that I was known to bless folks before journeys with something called Easter water and . . . I finished for him: Sure, I'd be glad to send you off with a blessing.

I took down the green, fish-shaped bottle that we refill at every Easter Vigil. We've used this water in the family for years to bless one another at important moments: Small children at bedtime, the bed itself, the house on Epiphany, animals, seeds, foods, computers — whatever needed it or whenever we needed it. I'd always tried to lift these blessings out of the realm of magic and bring us back to mystery — the mystery of our baptism into the Body of Christ.

I am seriously squirrely about anything that smacks of superstition. Superstition seems so fueled by fears and hopes for easy and magical solutions, while sacred rituals open us to mystery and renew our purpose and fix us in love. How could I explain to Dana the nature of Easter water? I didn't even know if Dana was baptized. I had the grace — to explain nothing.

I made a large wet cross on his forehead, and holding his hands, I prayed that he would find his family well. That they would enjoy one another. That he would catch lots of fish and see plenty of birds in his binoculars. That no snakes would bite him or alligators eat him up. That, indeed, he would be kept safe on this journey which was but a small reflection of his life journey. And may he continue to live (as he had once told me was his desire) as Jesus might live — say, like, if Jesus were going fishing in Texas. Something like that . . . and Dana's face was a bit wetter than any Easter water had made it. I then walked him back to his car, when he hesitated again, nodding toward his "little rice grinder" as he called it: Could you?

Sure. And I flung a long splash across the hood of his car. To which he answered: All *right!* Right *on!* And then he left.

Now he stood here again: "I'm back!" he smiled broadly. "It worked just great. Thirty-seven miles to the gallon going and forty-two coming back! But you know that Easter water? I just couldn't wash it off until I was three-quarters back home, and you know how that worked? By now the car was crusty with those little black flies, and when I stopped for a hamburger, there were these guys who held up a sign: Car Wash. Three dollars. They were these big — really big — black men and I told them I was sorry they'd have to work so hard on this one for only three bucks. I ate my hamburger sitting on a bench watching them, and I was drawing them in that little sketch book you gave me and thinking about what was happening to my Easter water. And then — know what they told me? They were so nice. They told me they were in this gospel choir and they were earning the money to get some golden choir robes! Man! Then I knew it was all going to be okay that they washed that Easter water off. That was the only way it could've been done. That wash water of theirs was just another kind of Easter water, I figured. That water, and the swamp water — which *was* full of alligators by the way! — all this water is just boiling with God. I get so happy by that thought!"

So, then, when we have forgotten our longing or cannot name it, our rituals may begin as actions driven by fear—incantations and offerings to appease the unknown powers, to drive back alligators, to keep us moving in traffic or get us good mileage. These are the rites that keep us safe in the liminal periods life brings. And then through just this earthy experience, we move beyond the magic incantations and the fear into mystery and love. As a new people, we know now, that the darkness we fear is not outside us but is our own blindness to what is brightly transfigured before us. Perfectly simple. Infinitely rich.

"It is this earthy spirituality that Christians need to recover," says theologian Rosemary Haughton, "if the church is to be prophetic, wild and holy, and not merely socially enlightened. It is time to take the lid once more off the well of truth from which the mystics and saints drew."

Song, story, sign, gesture, candlelight, the incense-offering are all the stuff of rites that we do not need to invent but are already our as humans. The stuff to set us straight, to reaffirm and bless the human condition is the stuff we bring in our hands. The matter, *materia,* of ordinary things, we ourselves and in the flesh, are imbued with the sacred—God-with-us.

In our hands, even now, lies a sign we use as Christians, so often and just as often so poorly—without awareness. It is the sign of the cross. Here is what Guardini invites us to remember about this sign and how to make it:

> You can make the sign of the cross and make it rightly. Nothing in the way of a hasty waving of the hand from which no one could understand what you are doing—no, a real sign of the cross: slow, large, from forehead to breast, and from one shoulder to the other. Don't you feel that it takes in the whole of you? Gather up all thoughts and all feeling into this sign as it goes from forehead to breast. Pull yourself together, as it goes from shoulder to shoulder. It covers the whole of you, body and soul; it gathers you up, dedicates you, sanctifies you.
>
> Why? Because it is the sign of the whole person and the sign of redemption. On the cross, Christ redeemed all persons. Through the cross he sanctifies the whole of us, down to the very last fiber of our being.

Gertrud Mueller Nelson

That is why we cross ourselves before our prayers, so that the sign may pull us together and set us in order, may fix thoughts, heart and will in God. After prayers we cross ourselves, so that what God has given us may stay with us. In temptation, that it may strengthen us, in danger, that it may protect us; when a blessing is given, that the fullness of life from God may be taken into our soul, and may consecrate all in it and make it fruitful.

Think of this when you make the sign of the cross. It is the holiest sign there is. Make it carefully, slowly; make a large one, with recollection. For then it embraces your whole being, body and soul, your thoughts and your will, imagination and feeling, doing and resting; and in it all will be strengthened, stamped, consecrated in the power of Christ, in the name of the Holy Trinity. (Romano Guardini, *Sacred Signs* [London: Sheed and Ward, 1937]: 3)

Let us close our evening with the sign of the cross: In the name of the Father, and of the Son and of the Holy Spirit. Amen.

Authors

Anscar J. Chupungco, OSB, is president of the Pontifical Liturgical Institute in Rome and director of the Paul VI Institute of Liturgy in the Philippines. He is the author of numerous books and articles on liturgy and liturgical inculturation.

Mary Collins, OSB, is professor of liturgical studies in the religion and religious education department at Catholic University of America. She was honored in 1995 with the Michael Mathis award in recognition of her valued contributions to the renewal of worship in the North American church.

Michael S. Driscoll, a presbyter of the diocese of Helena, Montana, is assistant professor of theology and liturgy at the University of Notre Dame. He holds doctorates in theology with a specialization in liturgy and sacramental theology from L'Institut Catholique de Paris, and in religious studies from the Sorbonne (Paris).

Mark R. Francis, CSV, holds a doctorate in sacred liturgy from the Pontifical Liturgical Institute of Saint Anselm in Rome and is associate professor of liturgy at Catholic Theological Union in Chicago. He is author of *Liturgy in a Multicultural Community* and coauthor of *Primero Dios: Hispanic Liturgical Resource.*

James M. Hayes, native, priest and archbishop emeritus of Halifax, Nova Scotia, participated in the final session of Vatican II as a Council Father. He served as archbishop of Halifax for twenty-five years and was a member of the episcopal board of the International Committee on English in the Liturgy from 1975–78.

Theresa F. Koernke, IHM, assistant professor of theology at Washington Theological Union, holds appointments in the word and worship department and the department of systematic and moral theology. She is a popular lecturer and focuses on contemporary issues related to eucharist.

Nathan D. Mitchell is associate director for research at the Notre Dame Center for Pastoral Liturgy and editor of its publications, *Assembly* and *Liturgy Digest*. He is a prolific writer and is well known for his provocative commentary in *Worship* magazine's Amen Corner.

J-Glenn Murray, SJ, director of the Office of Worship for the diocese of Cleveland, is a popular lecturer and author. He is the editor of a bimonthly African American liturgical newsletter, *Plenty Good Room*.

Gertrud Mueller Nelson, artist, psychologist and liturgist, speaks and writes about Christian life and worship. Among the first "clip-artists," she is well known for her refreshing insights into the meaning of human life through creative storytelling.

Thomas F. O'Meara, OP, a priest of the Central Province of the Dominican Order, is the William K. Warren Professor of Theology at the University of Notre Dame. Widely published, he received the John Courtney Murray Award in 1991 from the Catholic Theological Society.

Helen Marie Raycraft, OP, a member of the Sinsinawa Dominican Congregation, ministers among Hispanics in evangelization and the formation of basic ecclesial communities. At present, she serves on the Dominican Missionary Preaching Team based in Austin, Texas.

Sylvia L. Sanchez has served as the vice president of the Instituto de Liturgia Hispana. She currently works within the Hispanic community as a liturgy workshop facilitator, catechist for her parish RCIA program, and producer and host of Spanish programming for the diocesan radio station.

Julia Upton, RSM, is professor of theology at St. John's University, New York, and director of its Center for Teaching and Learning. Her publications include *Becoming a Catholic Christian* and *A Church for the Next Generation.*

Catherine Vincie, RSHM, is a liturgical theologian who focuses on the liturgical renewal of Vatican II. Her interest in communities ritualizing their efforts to be "a church in the modern world" has led her to bring issues of justice, women's concerns, inculturation and ecology to her work.